AF564763

A.K. CHETTIAR (1911–1983) was a pioneering documentary film-maker and the founder-editor of the Tamil journal *Kumari Malar* (1943–1983). The journal specialised in documenting the social and cultural history of Tamilnadu. An acclaimed travel writer, he studied photography in Tokyo and New York.

A.R. VENKATACHALAPATHY is a social historian. He is Professor at the Madras Institute of Development Studies, Chennai. He has published widely in Tamil, and is also the author of *In Those Days there was no Coffee: Writings in Cultural History* and the translator of Sundara Ramaswamy's *J.J.: Some Jottings*.

S. THILLAINAYAGAM is Professor of English at Manonmaniam Sundaranar University, Tirunelveli. The author of *Feminist Literary Essays*, he is currently translating Mylai. Seeni. Venkatasamy's *Buddhism in the Tamil Country*.

In the Tracks of the Mahatma

Gandhi Studies

The life and thought of Mahatma Gandhi are intertwined and inseparable. His politics was imbued with his spiritual experiments and his spirituality was tempered by his vision of a non-violent society, and his constructive work was integral to his politics. The unique practices of Gandhi, his control of palate, his fasts, his spinning, his silence and his prayers were as much a part of his politics as of his spiritual life. These practices and experiments were sustained and nurtured by the ashrams that he founded. The ashram community through its own practices affirmed, modified and validated Gandhi's ideals and practices.

Gandhi Studies aspires to examine and elucidate the relationship between life and thought, between experiment and practice, and between Gandhi and the institutions he founded and the experiments he inspired. Biographical studies of Gandhi and his associates, histories of institutions and ideas, along with translations of scholarly and memoir literature from various Indian languages would form part of this endeavour. This series is committed to no one fixed way of understanding Gandhi; it hopes like Gandhi himself to be deeply dialogic.

New titles

Harilal Gandhi: A Life, C.B. Dalal (Trans. Tridip Suhrud)
In the Tracks of the Mahatma: The Making of a Documentary, A.K. Chettiar (Ed. A.R. Venkatachalapathy; Trans. S. Thillainayagam)

Forthcoming titles

My Life is My Message: A Biography of Mahatma Gandhi, Narayan Desai, 4 volumes (Trans. Tridip Suhrud)
Non-violent Relationality: Rethinking Gandhi in the World, (Ed. Debjani Ganguly and John Docker)

In the Tracks of the Mahatma: The Making of a Documentary

A.K. CHETTIAR

Edited and introduced
by
A.R. VENKATACHALAPATHY

Translated from the Tamil *Annal Adichuvattil*
by
S. THILLAINAYAGAM

Orient Longman

ORIENT LONGMAN PRIVATE LIMITED

Registered Office
3-6-752 Himayatnagar, Hyderabad 500 029 (A.P.), India
Email: cogeneral@orientlongman.com

Other Offices
Bangalore, Bhopal, Bhubaneshwar, Chennai
Ernakulam, Guwahati, Hyderabad, Jaipur, Kolkata,
Lucknow, Mumbai, New Delhi, Patna, Pune

First published 2006

The Tamil original of *In the Tracks of the Mahatma* (*Annal Adichuvattil*) was compiled and edited by A.R. Venkatachalapathy and first published in 2003 by Kalachuvadu Pathippagam, Nagercoil.

ISBN 13: 978-81-250-3142-0
ISBN 10: 81-250-3142-1

Typeset by
Universal Print Systems Limited
Chennai 600 008

Printed in India at
SS Colour Impression Private Limited
Chennai 600 106

Published by
Orient Longman Private Limited
160 Anna Salai
Chennai 600 002
Email: chegeneral@orientlongman.com

Contents

Editor's Introduction

October 2, 1937. Aboard the *Samaria*, travelling from New York to Dublin, a 26-year-old man dreamed of making a documentary on the life of Mahatma Gandhi. Over the next two and a half years he travelled across the world – some 100,000 miles – with the Second World War looming large, and its outbreak jeopardising his search. He collected 50,000 feet of footage, shot by a hundred different cameramen over three decades and across four continents. He edited this into a 12,000-foot documentary and released it in August 1940 with Tamil commentary, and a few months later, with Telugu commentary. Fearing government repression and possible confiscation, the film then went into hiding. On 14 August 1947, the film was screened in New Delhi as celebrations rent the air. In 1948 he made this film in Hindi as well. A few years later, in 1952–53, he re-edited the film with English commentary in Hollywood (at the height of the McCarthy era) and screened it in the United States of America. *In the Tracks of the Mahatma* is the story of the making of this documentary in the words of the man who achieved this stupendous task: A.K. Chettiar (1911–1983).

~

A.K. Chettiar was a modest and self-effacing man. And therefore, it is difficult to reconstruct his life.[1] He left behind no account of his life. Even among his

---

1. Sa. Kandaswamy's Tamil monograph (*A.K. Chettiar*, Delhi: Sahitya Akademi, 2000) in the Sahitya Akademi's Makers of Indian Literature series is the only work on A.K. Chettiar. It is an inadequate work and he draws much of his information, without suitable acknowledgment, from a tribute by A.K. Chettiar's close associate S. Gopalan (written under the pseudonym 'Nanban') in *Kumari Malar* (September 1983), published shortly after his death. The information provided by Gopalan forms the basis of the notes provided by Somalay (*Chettinadum Sentamilum*, Chennai: Vanathi Pathippagam, 1984/1999) and the Nattukkottai Chettiar compendium, *Nagarathar Kalaikkalanjiam* (Chennai: Manivasagar Pathippagam,

friends, who number quite a few, he seems to have been reticent about the details of an eventful and productive life. We do not even know the names of his parents or his wife. This life-sketch is thus pieced together from bits of information gleaned from his various writings, obituary notices and tributes, and conversations with, and reminiscences of, his friends.

Annamalai Karuppan Chettiar was born in the Nattukkottai Chettiar community, known for its business enterprise and shrewd commercial acumen. As South and Southeast Asia were opened up for colonial exploitation in the nineteenth century, Nattukkottai Chettiars entered its financial markets – in Ceylon, Burma, Malaya, Indo-China, Sumatra, Thailand, etc. – and gained windfall profits. The massive mansions that litter the Chettinadu landscape offer the most striking testimony to their wealth. A significant presence in the economic and social life of Tamilnadu, they won great fame with their philanthropic activities, endowments to temples, and patronage of arts and literature.

On 4 November 1911, A.K. Chettiar was born in the small village of Kottaiyur in the Chettinadu region in central Tamilnadu. Even this date comes to us as American immigration officials interrogate him when he enters the United States of America in 1952 for remaking his film on Gandhi in Hollywood.

> The officer dictated the particulars to the typist. In my application, I had indicated my date of birth as 4–11–1911. He read it out as 11 April 1911. I intervened and said that I was born on 4 November 1911.
>
> The officer was taken aback at my objecting to my date of birth. "Isn't that what you have written?" he asked.
>
> "What I've written is correct. But you have read it wrongly." I explained the difference between the Indian and American ways of marking dates. "We write the day first; you write the month first. I was not born on 11 April, but on 4 November."

1998). R. Muthukumaraswamy, in an unsigned obituary (*Sentamil Selvi*, September 1983), also provides some details on A.K. Chettiar.

As mentioned earlier, we do not even know the names of his parents. In an essay on the famed temple town of Thiruvannamalai, he remarks that he spent eight years in school and twenty-four days in prison while in that town. It is characteristic that we do not know why exactly he went to prison, except for the fact that it was in the cause of the nation. He briefly mentions his imprisonment, in what is to us a tantalising reference, while he is interrogated by the American immigration officials.

Q: Have you ever been to jail?
A: Yes.
Q: Why?
A: I did not wish to. But the then British government put me in jail.
Q: Why?
A: For political reasons.

After schooling, he returned to his hometown at the age of sixteen. Even as a young man he was interested in reading periodicals. Since his uncle, his father's elder brother, subscribed to the nationalist daily *Swadesamitran*, he read it regularly. Apart from the Tamil journals that he borrowed from his friends, we also know that he subscribed to two English journals: *To-day*, edited by M.S. Kamath, and the *Doodle*. It was during this period that he met and spent a few days with Boothur Vaidyanatha Iyer, the founder of *Ananda Vikatan,* who had come on a subscription-raising tour of Chettinadu for his newly founded *Ananda Vijaya Vikatan.*[2] This was not surprising, considering that Chettinadu was known for supporting cultural and social activities; in fact, by the turn of the 1930s, it was a major centre of Tamil publishing—of both books and journals. The epicentre of much frenetic social activity, no major social movement was without its fervent supporters among the Chettiars.

In late 1930, and not yet twenty years old, A.K. Chettiar began to edit a monthly journal *Dhanavanigan* (another name of his community)

2. Boothur Vaidyanatha Iyer founded the *Ananda Vikatan* in 1926. After selling this journal to S.S. Vasan in 1928, he launched the *Ananda Vijaya Vikatan.*

from his hometown Kottaiyur. His name appears as the managing editor with an editorial board of five young persons some of whom, especially V.Rm. Chettiar, went on to become prominent in later days. Eight issues, one of them a double number, were published until 1931. A special number was published in November 1932 and we have no further information on it—surely it must have died. Prominent among *Dhanavanigan*'s contributors were the Tamil scholar, Pandithamani M. Kathiresan Chettiar, and the women's activist Dr. Muthulakshmi Reddi. The contents of the journal were broad, though we find some notes on the abolition of untouchability and an essay (probably translated) on Mahatma Gandhi. In an interesting article, A.K. Chettiar himself talks about the growing schisms within the Chettiar community caused by the growth of various social and political movements—events that left their mark on him. I found a reference to his having attended the first Self-Respect marriage[3] – that of Neelavathi, a Naidu and Ramasubramanian, a Chettiar – in the Chettinadu region, organised personally by Periyar E.V. Ramasamy. Considering that this event was highly controversial and a cause celebre of the time, his attendance at the marriage may be seen as making a political point. However, it must be noted that A.K. Chettiar maintained a distance from, as well as a near silence on, the Dravidian movement. His life-long interest in Gandhi probably dates from this time, though there is no record of his initiation in any of his own writings. It is likely that A.K. Chettiar was still in Thiruvannamalai when Gandhi visited Chettinadu in 1927; during Gandhi's subsequent visit to Chettinadu in 1934, he was in Burma. Probably, he absorbed Gandhism from his wide reading and the zeitgeist of the time.

After his first foray into the world of journalism, probably in late 1933, A.K. Chettiar left for Rangoon, Burma. It is said that the purpose of this relocation was to take over a journal, once again called *Dhanavanigan,* an organ of the Burma Nattukkottai Nagarathar Sangam. Two of the three Pongal

---

3. Self-Respect marriages emphasised the contractual nature of marriage and did away with priests and vedic rituals. Periyar E.V. Ramasamy and the Dravidian movement advocated this form of marriage from the late 1920s.

special numbers of *Dhanavanigan* (dated 1934 and 1936), which I have seen, identify A.Rm.A. Karuppan Chettiar as the editor. The 1937 issue lists a different name. It is reasonable to assume that A.K. Chettiar edited this journal for a little over two years, between end 1933 and mid 1936. In the 1936 Pongal issue he had authored a long essay, with a number of photographs, on the press in Japan. This was to form the basis for his first book, one of the many travelogues that he was to write, *Japan*, published from Rangoon in 1936. (This book was banned by the British Indian government in 1942 as Japan entered the war against the Allies.)

It was during these years, 1936 and 1937, that he was formally trained in photography at the Imperial College of Photography, Tokyo, and the New York Institute of Photography, New York. We know nothing about how he got admission and the details of his training.

Sometime earlier, probably before he left Chettinadu for Burma, he got married. It is said that it was a marriage of compulsion and that it was never consummated. We do not know the name of his wife. He was known to be silent about this particular event in his life. He is also said to have legally severed all ties with his family.

~

The events described in this book pertain to this phase of his life. The new medium of the moving image had begun to capture the imagination of the people as well as the intellectuals. This was also the time when the capital of the Nattukkottai Chettiars, fleeing from Southeast Asia, was being channelled into films.[4] Even though profits were the last thing on A.K. Chettiar's mind, this must certainly have provided the context for the production of the Gandhi film. His interest in the art of photography in conjuncture with his commitment to Gandhi led to the making of the film.

---

4. The Chettiars were fleeing in the wake of the uncertain economic situation following the Great Depression and the imminence of a world war; this situation was further heightened by the resistance of the local people to the rapacious and usurious nature of their business activities.

In 1943, after the phenomenal critical success of his film on Gandhi, he founded a monthly, *Kumari Malar*, a journal he edited almost uninterruptedly for about forty years (1943–83). To circumvent the government restriction on starting new periodicals due to the severe paper shortage during the Second World War, he began to issue *Kumari Malar* as a serially numbered monthly publication modelled on the lines of *Penguin New Writing*—an innovation followed by many until the restrictions were removed. In its first phase, *Kumari Malar* published original articles by the leading writers and intellectuals of the time. In its second phase, a decade or so later, *Kumari Malar* reinvented itself as a journal specialising in documenting the social and cultural history of Tamilnadu. A.K. Chettiar rummaged through old collections of books and journals and reprinted articles and news items that threw light on the history of modern Tamilnadu.[5] His special focus was on the role of Tamilnadu in the Indian freedom struggle.

Apart from reproducing information of the early, pre-Gandhian phase of the national movement, A.K. Chettiar did stellar work in collecting information about Gandhi in Tamil journals from before he became known as the Mahatma.[6] Documents pertaining to Gandhian social reform activity – the anti-untouchability campaign, the temperance movement, khadi and basic education programme – occupy considerable space in the journal.[7] Subramania Bharati was rather close to his heart and *Kumari Malar* made a major contribution to the efforts to compile his scattered and uncollected works. A.K. Chettiar also had special respect for Rajaji, who was accorded significant space in the pages of *Kumari Malar*.

---

5. Apart from documenting the history of Tamilnadu from such journals, he was especially generous in donating volumes of these journals to Maraimalai Adigal Library, Chennai; to Roja Muthiah, the famed antiquarian of Chettiar's home-town, whose collections are now housed in a library in Chennai named after him; and to the library of B. Krishnamurthy, Pudukkottai.
6. Later, A.K. Chettiar brought together these pieces to form a book. Two more volumes were to have followed, but they never saw the light of day.
7. His one blind spot was the Dravidian movement. There is scarcely a mention in his writings or in *Kumari Malar* about the social reform activities associated with the Dravidian movement.

A.K. Chettiar's other interests were travel and the history of Tamil journalism. He reproduced extracts and essays of travel writing from both within and outside Tamilnadu. (Later he also collected and edited a volume of these travel writings.) He innovatively reproduced the first editorials of old Tamil journals. He devoted a special issue to G. Subramania Iyer, the doyen of Indian journalism and a founder of the *Hindu* and the *Swadesamitran*, the earliest newspapers in English and Tamil respectively. He also published R.A. Padmanabhan's series on the history of Tamil journalism. A.K. Chettiar was also fascinated by the incursions of new artefacts into Tamil social life—coffee, new locomotives, electric lights, etc. and the spread of new diseases such as plague and cholera. And he took delight in culling out news about them. It may be no exaggeration to say that monographs could be written on many aspects of Tamil cultural history based on the documentation found in *Kumari Malar* alone.

In the Tamil world, A.K. Chettiar is chiefly remembered as an artful practitioner of the travelogue—he is popularly known as *Ulagam Suttrum Tamilan*, 'the Tamil who travels around the world', after the title of one of his well-known books. In the late 1930s and the early 1940s, he wrote a number of articles on the travels that flowed from his search for original documentary footage on Gandhi. Of the dozen travelogues that he published, mention can be made of *America, America Naattil* (In America), *Prayana Ninaivugal* (Memories of Travels), *Malaya muthal Canada varai* (From Malaya to Canada), and *Caribbean Kadalum Guyanavum* (The Caribbean Sea and Guyana). He also wrote *Kudagu*, a book on Coorg. A.K. Chettiar travelled far and wide at a time when it was not common for Tamils to venture abroad. Believing that one should write about a place only after living in it for at least some years, he was careful not to be judgemental about other cultures.[8]

A.K. Chettiar died on 10 September 1983 at the house of his friend M. Deivarayan, on Vijayaraghavachari Road, Thiagaraya Nagar, Chennai.

---

8. Notably, he refused to permit the reprinting of his travelogues, maintaining that they had become dated.

He was two months short of his seventy-second birthday. No relatives were present when he was cremated in the Thiruvottriyur cremation ground.

~

The making of the Gandhi documentary film is the stuff of legends—a remarkable achievement by any standard. While he did refer and allude to the making of the film in some of his writings, it was not until 1978 that he brought himself to write a 10-part series in *Kumari Malar* on the making of the documentary.

Anecdotes include how he traced the footage on Tilak's funeral, including a few close-up shots of his face, filmed by Dadasaheb Phalke, acclaimed as the 'father' of Indian cinema, and the footage on Gandhi in South Africa during Gokhale's 1912-visit preserved carefully by H.S.L. Polak; an account of filming Romain Rolland in his French countryside retreat; and how he narrowly missed shooting C.F. Andrews. The narrative also teems with prominent personalities such as C. Vijayaraghavachariar, Madan Mohan Malaviya, Rajaji, S. Radhakrishnan, Jawaharlal Nehru, Madame Montessori and Acharya Kripalani. Also included are accounts of A.K. Chettiar's experiences of shooting on location in racist South Africa, his filming of activities in the Wardha Ashram, his experiences with the various film companies in Britain, the USA, Fascist Italy and much of the Continent as he went scouting for documentary footage.

There is much talk in Tamil circles about the Gandhi film being lodged here or there. For a long time it was believed that A.K. Chettiar had deposited the film at the National Film Archives, Pune. But S. Theodore Baskaran, the pioneering historian of Tamil cinema, states that the film is not to be found there. According to Baskaran, one clip from the film, the famous mass-spinning scene, included in a documentary on Martin Luther King, is the only portion that has survived. Even in Devadas Gandhi's essay on his project – as chairman of the Gandhi Films Committee of the Gandhi Smarak Nidhi – to preserve documentaries of Gandhi, he makes but one bare mention of A.K. Chettiar's pioneering attempt.[9] In the absence of the actual documentary, which runs to about two hours, A.K. Chettiar's *Annal Adichuvattil*, translated here, offers the only reliable account, apart from the English version of the film and contemporary reviews, of what went into the film.[10]

The text of *Annal Adichuvatil* carries the imprint of the personality that made the film. It has the same self-effacing quality characteristic of its author. Whenever an achievement is narrated, A.K. Chettiar uses 'we'; but when it comes to failings, he invariably claims responsibility with an 'I'. Written in the form of short episodes and vignettes, he details his experiences in a fascinating and riveting manner. His style is simple and direct, and profuse with punctuation. Little incidents and episodes are joined together in a garland. There is no grand narrative framing the text. The structure of the ten-part series is non-linear, consciously deflecting the reader's attention away from the achievements of the narrator.

Apart from being an account of the making of a film, this book also exemplifies a certain Gandhian spirit. Its narrative of the technical difficulties involved in the shooting and retrieving of archival footage and in post-production work, and the fact that it was one of the earliest attempts at making a documentary in India, also makes it a contribution to film history and film studies.[11]

---

9. "Documentary Films on Mahatma Gandhi", based on two talks on All India Radio.
10. As this book goes to the press, I was able to trace an abridged version of the 1953 Hollywood version. The film titled *Mahatma Gandhi: Twentieth Century Prophet*, re-edited in 1998 from the original length of 81 minutes to 45 minutes, is a reminder of A.K. Chettiar's great effort. This abridged version contains many of the sequences narrated by A.K. Chettiar in this book. The title cards authenticate his account of its remaking. (See Appendix 2.) The wide media coverage given to the recovery of the film, especially in the *Hindu*, has inspired further searches. A. Annamalai, director of the Gandhi Study Centre, Chennai, following this lead, has traced the presence of the complete 1953 English version in the Gandhi Peace Foundation, Madurai.
11. It should be remembered that, way back in 1943, A.K. Chettiar had published a book of essays on cinema, *Thiraiyum Vazhvum*, Chennai.

In the Tracks of the Mahatma is translated from the Tamil version edited by A.R.Venkatachalapathy and published in late 2003 by Kalachuvadu Pathippagam, Nagercoil. It reproduces in book form, for the first time, the ten-part account of the making of the documentary serialised in *Kumari Malar* between June 1978 and April 1979. An essay published in 1943 in A.K. Chettiar's *Thiraiyum Vazhvum* has been employed as the prologue. His essay in *Kumari Malar*, April 1978, on the screening of the film in New Delhi on the eve of Indian independence has been included in this book as Appendix 1. Portions from his *America Nattil* (1956), on the remaking of the film in English in Hollywood forms Appendix 2. His essay on S. Radhakrishnan published in *Kumari Malar*, May 1978, has been added at the end of Chapter 3. Similarly, his essay on Romain Rolland, published in his *Ulagam Suttrum Tamilan,*[12] has been interpolated at the appropriate place in Chapter 5.

The English translation by S. Thillainayagam attempts to capture the tone of the original. Every effort has been made by the editor to identify the English spellings of names of people and places figuring in the original. As far as possible original quotations have been identified and used rather than having them retranslated back from Tamil. A.K. Chettiar uses the memorable phrase from Bharati's poem on Gandhi, *'Vazhga Nee Emman'* (Long live our Lord/Leader/Father) as a refrain at the end of every episode (marked in the text as section breaks). It has been deleted from the translation as it sounds trite and does not work in English. For similar reasons, other such references and allusions to Bharati's poems have been removed. Some explanatory footnotes have also been provided by the editor.

Acknowledgments: T. Kovendhan, my earliest mentor, first introduced me to A.K. Chettiar's life and work when I was still a school-going student. B. Krishnamurthy and Dorothy Krishnamurthy opened up the vast treasures of their Gnanalaya Library, Pudukkottai, for my reference. Mr. Krishnamurthy also permitted me to read A.K. Chettiar's letters and shared with me his notes

12. A.K. Chettiar, *Ulagam Suttrum Tamilan*, Chennai: Kumari Malar 1945, 69–72.

on A.K. Chettiar. S. Theodore Baskaran provided the photograph of the famous mass-spinning scene from the Gandhi film. R.A. Padmanabhan, the renowned Bharati scholar, R. Muthukumaraswamy, managing director of Saiva Siddhanta Works Publishing Society, and D. Meiyappan, son of A.K. Chettiar's friend, M. Deivarayan, shared their memories. Ramachandra Guha, apart from providing me with Devadas Gandhi's essay, also encouraged me to work on the English version. He provided perceptive comments on this introduction and answered queries, as did Gopal Gandhi. Steve Hughes provided me with additional material. Kannan, of Kalachuvadu Pathippagam, provided unstinting support for the publication of the original Tamil volume on which this book is fully based. Maraimalai Adigal Library, Chennai, and Roja Muthiah Research Library, Chennai, permitted access to their holdings. As the book goes to press, Blake Wentworth and Whitney Cox, both doctoral students at the University of Chicago, helped me trace the abridged version of the Gandhi film made in Hollywood. I am especially grateful to Blake for his resourcefulness in tracing and contacting Doug Sharples, the producer of the 1998 abridged English version of the film. Don Lane, who had worked with Stanley Neal Productions in 1953 and Doug Sharples provided details about the making of the Hollywood version. S. Anand helped in identifying the film and searched out some additional information. Thanks are due to the *Hindu* and the associate editor of *Frontline*, T.S. Subramanian, for the extensive coverage of the recovery of the film which revived interest in the film. R. Sivapriya provided excellent editorial support. I remain grateful to them.

It is my lasting regret that a copy of the 1953 English version of the film could not be provided with this book due to prohibitive costs.

A.R. Venkatachalapathy
Chennai
February 2006

In the Tracks of the Mahatma

Prologue

October 2, 1937. I was travelling to Dublin from New York on the *Samaria*. That holy day – the birthday of the Mahatma – is familiar to all Indians.

Some friends had made arrangements to celebrate Gandhiji's birthday in New York. But I could not stay back for the festivities. While I was mourning the missed opportunity, an idea suddenly dawned on me. Why not celebrate it on the sea? The only other Indian aboard the ship agreed and I began making arrangements immediately.

A few American friends also joined us. It was a small and joyful occasion that concluded successfully with Indian food. After the celebration dinner, I went up to the deck to reflect awhile. I felt deeply moved thinking about how much the nation was indebted to the Mahatma, and the idea of producing a film originated like a flash in my mind. The thought kept me awake through the night: Why should I not make an authentic documentary on Gandhiji's life and experiences?

The moment I woke up, I rushed to my friend and described my plan. He laughed. But on seeing my earnestness, he agreed to discuss it with me. We talked for a long time and prepared a blueprint. That small piece of paper was the basis for the documentary on Gandhiji.

When the plan began to take shape, my friend too felt some belief in it. He conceded that it was indeed a good idea. Yet, he said, "It might be possible to produce a short film on Gandhiji. But how can you make a full-length film? All the available information on him will have to be collected. Is that feasible?"

"I will travel all over the world. I will visit every news agency. I will rummage through film heaps in every part of the world. I will look into every film library. I will accomplish this task at any cost," I replied.

But he did not look impressed.

I wandered all over Europe. On my return home, I went to the Haripura Congress. I visited all the studios in India and discussed my plan with innumerable producers, but to no avail.

Meanwhile, I received an offer from the largest studio in India to become the president of its proposed news division. Toying with this offer, I delayed the production of the documentary for some time. But when they abandoned the proposal, I returned to my original plan.

Most of the film producers in Chennai laughed at my project. Some could not even understand it. The manager of a film company told the proprietor in my presence, "People won't come to see a documentary even if it is screened for free."

Many thought I was a dreamer, building castles in the air; they felt that I was a confused young man entertaining impractical ideas as a result of my travels to foreign countries. In the midst of all this, a few producers requested me to direct their films, and the fat salaries they offered were tempting. But I vowed to myself that I would not give up my plan.

It was after all these difficulties that 'Documentary Films Limited' was started. It took almost a year for the company to begin functioning. During this time, I had the opportunity to get to know the Tamil producers fairly well. But I still clung to my plan like a madman.

I went up and down India many times. Within a period of five months I had visited more than half of the world on fast ships and aeroplanes.

The task of collecting old footage was very interesting, especially in India. When I scouted for old footage that would be useful for my film in Indian studios, many looked at me with astonishment. They asked me, "What are you going to do with this rubbish?" But it was in that rubbish that I found rare treasures!

The shots I collected in the first year were not enough for a full-length film. So, I went to Europe.

I visited more than thirty documentary companies in the United States of America and Europe. Both in eastern and western countries I collected shots pertaining to Gandhiji's life. Collecting stock shots abroad was far easier and cheaper than in India.

In most of the countries there are documentary companies and film libraries. On receiving a specific enquiry, they look into their list of films and answer in minutes whether the required film is available with them. In most places, I could complete my work within twenty-four hours.

In London, I called on Henry S.L. Polak, a friend of the Mahatma. As I was explaining my project to him, he casually opened an old tin box and showed me the positive copy of a very old film of about two hundred feet length. He said that it was a historically important film, and that he had kept it safe for twenty-seven years. When we were viewing it on the screen after making a copy of it, Polak explained, "This film was taken when the late Gopal Krishna Gokhale visited South Africa. You can see Mahatma Gandhi in a European suit." Undoubtedly, this film is one of the rarest historical documents of our country. Can anyone imagine that in 1912, in a South Africa that was not yet developed, they could have produced a film—that too, on Gandhi and Gokhale? It was a greater fortune that Polak had preserved it so carefully and presented it to us. He is none other than the same Polak who stood shoulder to shoulder with Gandhiji in all his struggles in South Africa. We are forever indebted to Polak for having preserved this rare treasure and gifting it to India.

In England, I did not get much cooperation from the British news agencies. In one news agency, they demanded a pound for every foot of film! When I was ready to pay even that incredibly exorbitant price, they refused to sell. They said that the film on Gandhiji's visit to London had political overtones and that I might use it in a manner prejudicial to the interests of their government. Therefore, they would not sell it to me for any amount. I had to actually buy parts of those films in other countries after much arduous search.

In France, film companies helped me whole-heartedly. The assistance rendered by Éclair Drass was especially useful. The happiest part of the journey was the few days I spent with Romain Rolland at his birthplace Vezeley. He spent six months of every year there. He did not know English, so I could communicate with him only through his wife.

Romain Rolland was the first great man to write a biography of Gandhiji and introduce him to the world at large. Initially, he refused to give his opinions on Gandhiji on camera because he thought that his face was not photogenic! At last, after much persuasion and his wife's pleading, he consented. At once, I telephoned Charles Martin, the famous documentary cinematographer, and asked him to come to Rolland's house. The next morning, Romain Rolland's words on the Mahatma were recorded.

After completing the collection of footage in Europe, I set sail to America by *Pidsuski*, the Polish ship that was sunk by its enemies in the early days of the war.

In New York, my old friends welcomed me warmly. My second visit to that city was brief. Many news agencies came forward to cooperate with me. Freehaver of the New York Public Library took great efforts on my behalf and put together the two hundred odd books on Gandhiji written in several European languages. I enlisted the help of an expert American cinematographer and filmed this treasure. In the Library of Congress at Washington, they helped me film the large number of books available on Gandhiji.

I had to leave America immediately. As I had absolutely no spare time I was constrained to decline an invitation from Washington Radio to give a talk on my film. I had barely seven hours to look at the wonderful World Exhibition.

From America, the gigantic ship *Freeman* took me to Southampton. The next programme on my agenda – a visit to South Africa – proved to be tough. In no ship leaving England for South Africa was a berth available for an Indian. With great difficulty I managed to get a berth on a ship that supposedly had 'no vacancy'. But the scene I witnessed on board the ship astonished me! The passengers numbered just sixty-one! *Windsor Castle* weighed 20,000 tonnes. Its dining hall could accommodate two hundred people. But I was made to sit alone, separately. The other sixty passengers dined together. The special treatment accorded to me was no honour—it was an insult.

Not for a day or two—I had to endure these humiliations for thirteen and a half days. The insults did not cease even after reaching Cape Town. There, the railway officials told me that I would be served food only at my seat, I could not eat with others in the dining hall. Luckily, I could get a ticket on the Durban flight just half an hour hence. I reached Durban, 1200 miles away from Cape Town, in seven hours.

Tamils live in large numbers in South Africa. Yet, even today, Indians are not allowed to walk in certain streets of Durban. In buses and trams non-whites must confine themselves to the last three rows. Indians and blacks are herded into some buses like cattle! Banks have separate counters for Indians. There are even exclusive post offices! Indians are not allowed inside most of the theatres, hotels and restaurants. In Johannesburg I asked for soda water in a small shop. The saleswoman told me, "Nothing is available in a bottle." It was in this country that Mahatma Gandhi had stayed for more than twenty years and organised several struggles against these atrocities.

But even South Africa was not totally devoid of pleasant experiences. 'Gandhi' proved to be a magic word. That was the real ticket for entry! The Phoenix Settlement started by Gandhiji was still there. I met several workers and colleagues of Gandhiji who had stood shoulder to shoulder with him. I can never forget the incidents they narrated about the first satyagraha.

Hermann Kallenbach, a European architect settled in Johannesburg, was Gandhiji's friend. He carried on his shoulders the tripod of my camera for over half an hour when I shot the Tolstoy Farm! Such was his love for the Mahatma.

The war broke out when I was in Johannesburg. All shipping companies expressed their inability to accommodate me, declaring 'no vacancy'. One company said that it would not permit Indians to travel first class. I fought for my rights with the help of the agent general of the Indian government and the Chamber of Commerce, and eventually won.

After returning to India, I continued with my frantic search for new shots. Cameramen of various documentary companies waited in Wardha for months together. It is very difficult to film Gandhiji. He does not stand for a minute in front of a camera. Generally, he would walk very fast. Moreover, people would be standing around him all the time and would stretch their necks towards the camera hoping to get a snapshot with Gandhiji. Most cameramen were not admitted into Gandhiji's cottage. Despite these tremendous odds a few wonderful shots of Gandhiji's life have been recorded.

We produced a documentary of 12,000 feet from the 50,000 odd feet of film that we collected. It took about three years to bring it to this length.

I had travelled one lakh miles, more or less, and across four continents to collect the footage. The documentary is the result of films shot by nearly a hundred cameramen, in thirty years, all over the world. I believe that this is the first full-length historical film produced in the documentary tradition to present the life of an individual. If a full-length film is to be made on any individual in India, who else could be the appropriate subject, but the Mahatma?

~

In the history of the film on Mahatma Gandhi the names of the following great men should occupy an important place: Le. Natesan, Mu.Azha. Azhagappa Chettiar, Ka.Saa.A.A. Sambandam Chettiar, Guntur Narasimha Rao, P.V. Pathy, P. Subramaniam and Su.Veera. Veerappa Chettiar.

From *Thiraiyum Vazhvum* (1943)

1

They say 'means are after all means'. I would say 'means are after all everything'. As the means so the end. There is no wall of separation between means and end. Indeed the Creator has given us control (and that too very limited) over means, none over the end. Realisation of the goal is in exact proportion to that of the means. This is a proposition that admits of no exception.

Mahatma Gandhi

The Mahatma's life is often offered as an illustrious example in our country. But very few have adopted such a life as their goal. Among them, fewer still have achieved a modicum of success. It would be no exaggeration to say that it was possible for the Mahatma alone to adopt Gandhian principles and live by them.

In our personal lives we succumb to various desires and commit innumerable mistakes. Knowingly or unknowingly we persist in committing mistakes. But as far as the film on the Mahatma was concerned, we took a vow to follow Gandhian principles as far as possible. I am not sure of the extent of our success. We may have unintentionally committed mistakes. But whenever we realised that something was wrong, we desisted from proceeding with it.

This was due to our reverence for Gandhiji. We also felt fear, akin to the fear of god. We felt this reverential fear because we worshipped him as an incarnation of god.

~

When immersed in the sorrow of Gandhiji's death, Jawaharlal Nehru lamented, "Gandhiji raised all of us to a level we had never dreamt of. But after his death we reverted to the old condition, nay, we fell into an abysmal depth."

Dr. D.F. Karaka, the well-known writer, in his book on Gandhiji, *Out of Dust,* wrote, "Out of dust, he made us into men." It is absolutely true.

I am one among the countless men he made out of mere dust.

~

The beginning of 1940. We were very busy editing the film on Gandhiji. We who had been staying in a hotel until then, rented the ground floor of a new terraced building on College Road in Matunga, Bombay. The rent was forty rupees a month. The landlord did not live in the city and his friend who lived in the same street collected the rent. We sought him out every month to hand over the rent. Not once did he ask for it.

There was no table, chair or cot in the house. There was but one rickety folding chair, and even that belonged to the landlord. It was reserved for visitors who wore trousers.

One morning we decided to apply for a telephone connection. I went to the telephone office on Hornby Road and paid a deposit of fifteen rupees, after filling a form. The connection was provided before I returned home.

We hired a car on a monthly basis during our stay in Bombay. The rent was one hundred and fifty rupees. The owner of the car would pay the driver forty rupees as salary. We had to pay for the petrol. Petrol was rather cheap then. Our driver was a modest Goan Christian named Williams.

Our office did not have a nameplate. My assistant and I were based there. Our cinematographer, Dr. P.V. Pathy, and his crew lived in the area called Opera House. We met every day at the studio or elsewhere.

The old English nationalist daily, the *Bombay Chronicle,* was the leading newspaper then. Its editor, Syed A. Brelvi, was a patriot who had courted arrest several times. Coming out of the theatre, after having seen the film on Gandhiji, he embraced me.

Khwaja Ahmad Abbas had recently joined the *Bombay Chronicle* as an assistant editor. He wrote an excellent and lengthy article on the Gandhi film in the *Bombay Chronicle* and another special article in *Film India,* which was then a very popular magazine. He wrote in the *New York Times* as well. At the end of his piece, he wrote, "The producer of the Gandhi film has plans to rush to America as soon as the production is over and show it to the American President Roosevelt. Could this be the first Indian film ever seen by an American President?"

Because of these articles, news about the film spread, among the general public and the people connected with the film industry, in a dignified manner. Magazines published in various parts of India, in different Indian languages, carried articles on the Gandhi film.

~

One day, at about ten in the morning, a man came looking for me. He was short and bald, and around forty-five years old. Since he was wearing trousers, I asked him to sit on the rickety chair. He introduced himself, "My name is Ganpat Rao. I am the manager of the Bombay branch of the Twentieth Century Fox. I read about your Gandhi film in *Film India.* I went to your Chennai office to meet you. They said that you were in Bombay and gave me this address. Newberry, our general manager in India, would like to meet you. Can you come to our office? I will take you whenever it is convenient for you. We could even leave now, the car is round the corner."

Twentieth Century Fox is one of the biggest film companies in America. When I was in America, my Indian friend Ram Bagai had taken me to their studio a few times.

Since I did not have much work that day, I gave some instructions to my assistant and left with Ganpat Rao. While we were on our way, he told me, "Let's keep our discussion confidential, for now." I found his request puzzling.

Newberry was a young man from Australia. He greeted me with warmth, "I read the article on your Gandhi film. There is no doubt that you are a great salesman. One cannot find a better subject for a film. You need not produce any film for another ten years, this one film will do. Congratulations."

"I am interested in releasing this film in America through our company. It is enough if you give us the negative, we will provide an excellent background score, a commentary and everything else necessary, and release the film. After deducting the expenses we can share the profits equally between us. It will not be less than twenty lakhs, and your share will be no less than ten lakhs," said Newberry.

The moment he mentioned ten lakh rupees, my head began to reel. This was forty years ago, imagine its present value.

Somehow I managed to recover from the shock, "I cannot tell you anything decisively without consulting the directors of our company. We do not consider the film on Gandhiji a commodity—it is sacred to us. The commentary must be acceptable to us. It should have our approval."

Newberry replied, "I fully agree with you. First, I'll get a provisional acceptance from my company. We will submit to all your conditions regarding the commentary. We will also, as you have done, handle the film with reverence."

He wrote out a lengthy telegram, clearly stating all that he had said, and showed it to me. After getting my approval he made arrangements for wiring it to America.

He then added, "I have a request. A lot of effort and money is being invested in this project. It will be of help if you assure us, in writing, that for fifteen days from today you will not enter into any contract with anybody over your film."

"You can trust my word. But I will give an undertaking in writing for your sake." I handed over a typed letter to that effect and retained a copy for myself.

"Today, we have embarked on a great task. We must celebrate it. You must have lunch with us this afternoon," said Newberry. I agreed. "Shall we go to Hotel Ritz?" he asked. In those days, Ritz' fame was second only to that of Hotel Taj Mahal, and this was the British period—people dressed in vetti could get no respect in such places. They could even be insulted. I explained my hesitation to Newberry. He said, "You are my guest. Nothing untoward will happen. An insult to you would be a personal insult to me."

When we entered the Ritz, there were about sixty people in the dining hall. I turned around when I heard the words, "Hello, Mr. Chettiar. How are you?" It was the majestic voice of Madame Maria Montessori who was sitting at the head of the best table in the restaurant.

Madame Montessori was a teacher of world renown. I was dressed in Indian clothes, that too in khadi. So everyone looked at me with keen attention. I went to the Ritz hesitantly, fearing disrespect, but got a royal welcome!

~

Dr. Maria Montessori was an Italian. She was a genius who fully understood the love and enthusiasm bursting forth in young and tender minds. She herself was like a child, without a tinge of stealth or deceit. She had dedicated her whole life to the development of children's education. Her teaching method is known universally as the Montessori method. It has spread all over the world and helps in imparting education to children in a simple manner while keeping them happy.

Madame Montessori had come to Chennai on the invitation of the Theosophical Society to train teachers in her method of teaching. When she was in Chennai the Second World War broke out. Italy became an enemy country. Hence, the then British government imprisoned all Italians in India. Considering Madame Montessori's age, fame and work for the cause of education, it not only desisted from imprisoning her, but also allowed her several concessions so that she could continue her service to education.

Around Gandhiji's seventieth birthday, Dr. Radhakrishnan edited and published an anthology of rare value, entitled *Mahatma Gandhi,* consisting of essays from reputed scholars in various fields all over the world. It included an article by Madame Montessori. I considered her presence in Chennai at that time, a big fortune. I wished to film her speaking a few lines from that essay.

In pursuit of this, I went to Adyar where she was staying. There, a person called Shankara Menon stopped me and asked, "Why do you want to see Madame Montessori?" I answered him briefly. He began to cross-examine me persistently. His questions and his behaviour were disgusting. I looked at him sternly and said in a curt tone, "I have come to meet Madame Montessori, not you."

Madame Montessori welcomed me with a cheerful face and an innocent smile. I told her the purpose of my visit and requested her to speak a few lines on Gandhiji from her essay and also repeat them in Italian, her mother tongue.

Madame Montessori said, "Yours is a very good undertaking. I am ready to speak any time."

I fixed a date for the shooting in the following week. But two days before that I had to make an unexpected trip to Bombay. I made all arrangements, met Madame and informed her about everything. I strongly insisted that our manager be most respectful to that lady of exemplary character.

I came to know of all that happened during the filming only later.

The shooting took place on the appointed day. Madame Montessori spoke first in Italian, which was recorded.

She had to speak the same sentences in English. Generally, Europeans have difficulty in speaking English. Madame was no exception. If she read from the book, her face would not be seen clearly on the screen. So they wrote the two lines in very large letters on a black board and kept it at a distance for her to read.

> Every child in every corner of Europe knows Gandhi. When they see his picture, they exclaim in their own language, "O! This is Gandhi!"

Madame Montessori read them out. She could not pronounce the word 'exclaim' correctly. Every time she pronounced it wrong, she would burst into loud laughter like a child. This happened six times. Each time there was loss of film; loss of money. She pronounced it correctly the seventh time. It was a great blessing to record her words on film. Considering that, the loss was negligible.

~

When I met Madame Montessori at the Ritz all these came to my mind. I introduced Newberry and Ganpat Rao to her.

We took leave of her and had our dinner in another section of the hall. Newberry told me, "You were hesitant to come here. You feared insults.

I compelled you and brought you here, and thought I was doing you a favour. I even felt a sense of pride when I was leading you in. But see, how everything changed as soon as we entered this hall. Thanks to your kindness I have been introduced to a woman of international renown."

That night, I screened the Gandhi film exclusively for Newberry and Ganpat Rao in the little ten-seater theatre of the United Artists.

After watching the film, Newberry asked me, "Do you know why I sent the telegram to America before seeing the film?" I said that I did not. He said, "I sent the telegram earlier because I did not want to change my mind after seeing the film."

"All right. Now that you have seen the film, what do you think?" I asked.

"I hardly expected the film to be so good. Congratulations!"

Two days passed. Then a week. Two more weeks. Nothing happened. There was no reply from America. Everything was at a standstill.

Later, Newberry told me, "The telegram did not reach America. It seems the censoring authorities blocked it here. There was no use sending an airmail either. I am afraid that the government in India will not allow us to send the film on Gandhi abroad because of the political situation here. My dream castle has collapsed. I thank you wholeheartedly for your love and cooperation."

My dream castle too had crumbled to pieces. I could not bear this disappointment.

I realised later that it was God's will.

~

Two days later, a stranger came to see me. He said, "I heard certain things about your film on Gandhiji. If you agree, I can send it to America immediately."

"How?" I asked, rather eagerly.

"Next week, we are sending a lion to the Boston zoo from Goa by ship. We can hide the film reels under the lion's cage. The customs authorities of India will be scared to go near the lion. There will not be any problem in unloading the reels in America. We will deliver it at the address you give. Since it is a very risky affair you must pay us a handsome amount."

This was blatant smuggling. I should have refused it outright. But since desire lurked in my mind, I wavered.

The desire in my mind was not for money. I sincerely believed that this film could help create sympathy for the Indian independence struggle in America much as the squirrel helped the god Rama in building the bridge.

There was as much fear as there was desire. I did not know anything about this man. First, the directors of Documentary Films Limited must permit me to entrust him with the film. Perhaps they might permit me; but even then, I would not be able to get any acknowledgement from him for having received the film. After going to America he could sell the film to anybody. Then everything would be lost. The travails of so many years would go waste.

Desire and fear shook me alternately. Gandhiji's golden saying, "If means are not pure, the goal also will not be pure," disturbed my mind.

I prostrated before God for revealing the guiding light.

2

The year 1939. One morning, I saw a wonderful photograph – of about two hundred women, spinning with hand charkas, seated underneath trees – in the *Hindu*. Kovai A. Ayyamuthu had taken that mass-spinning photograph.

Ayyamuthu was a friend, a patriot and an able administrator. He was then the secretary of the Tamilnadu Khadi Board in Tiruppur. That was a time when Ayyamuthu meant khadi and khadi meant Ayyamuthu. He published a monthly called *Kudi Nool* just to promote the khadi movement. Ayyamuthu was also a talented photographer. The *Hindu* photograph had been taken in a village near Tiruppur.

When I met Ayyamuthu, I made a request, "Inform me when you organise another mass-spinning event. We would like to shoot it and include it in the Gandhi film."

"I'll organise an event for the sake of your film. It will also mean good publicity for the khadi movement," he said.

We fixed the dates for the shooting. It was the responsibility of the Khadi Board to bring people with hand charkas and supervise the spinning. We were to pay for the transport and bear the shooting expenses. It was to be a joint effort.

To Ayyamuthu's surprise, about two thousand women from three villages eagerly came forward to participate in the mass spinning. Though Ayyamuthu appeared tough, he had a kind heart. "Won't these poor women lose a day's wage? Every participant must be given a quarter rupee," he decided. He had indeed taken the right decision, but the Khadi Board should have paid the compensation.

Ayyamuthu wrote to us: "About five hundred rupees is required for us to be able to pay a quarter rupee to each woman. Send the amount."

It would cost us more than a thousand rupees to meet the transport, shooting and other expenses. Our financial position was not comfortable—it would be very difficult to raise even the thousand that was necessary.

Given such a situation, I refused to bear an expense that was unexpected and not previously agreed upon. So I wrote to Ayyamuthu to cancel the event.

Ayyamuthu replied by telegram: "All arrangements have been made. Shooting cannot be cancelled at this stage. Of the 500 rupees, the Khadi Board will bear half the amount; you bear the other half."

We accepted it as we had no choice.

On the appointed day we reached Tiruppur very early in the morning. Ayyamuthu and his men received us at the railway station. They had arranged two cars for our use. All of us went to the Khadi Board and Ayyamuthu kindly provided a good breakfast. We can never forget the loving hospitality extended to us by him, his wife and the Khadi Board employees throughout our stay.

We did the shooting in three villages, all of which wore a festive look. It was a marvellous sight—row after row of seated women, spinning en masse. Dr. Pathy was greatly enthused. Though he had no modern equipment, using all his skills and his artistic eye, he shot the scene from several perspectives. Most of the women did not even turn to look at the camera while they were spinning.

The shooting got over. But Dr. Pathy was doubtful about the effect of the continuously revolving charkas on film. He sent the negative for processing to Chennai through a messenger the same night. He requested the studio to send a telegram about the result.

The telegram gave us good news.

Then we filmed the day-to-day activities of the Khadi Board.

D.K. Pattammal sang *Aadu Raate* by Namakkal Kavignar Ramalingam Pillai for this sequence. The song was wonderfully appropriate.

The four hundred feet sequence, of two thousand women spinning their charkas, served to illustrate:

Ayyamuthu's organising capacity,
Dr. Pathy's expert photography,
Namakkal Kavignar's patriotic song, and
D.K. Pattammal's sweet voice!

It was Gandhiji, the kinsman of the poor, who revived the charka and succeeded in showing the way for thousands of honest women starving in villages to live independently, and without losing their honour!

~

In 1936, I was studying in Japan, staying in the YMCA building in an area called Kanta in Tokyo.

One day, a middle-aged Indian introduced himself to me in the dining hall. He was none other than Lt. Col. Dr. Mirajkar, one of India's well-known surgeons. He was born in Maharashtra and he worked in Lahore.

A little later, a lady from Tamilnadu joined us. The three of us had a light meal. The lady was Dr. Pichamuthu, a well-known doctor and patriot, from Panthadi Street, Madurai.

The two doctors were on a global tour and had stopped at Japan on their way back home from America. I was of some help to them during the two or three days of their stay.

While departing, Dr. Mirajkar gave me his card and asked me to get in touch with him if I ever visited Lahore.

"Indians who come here give us their cards and ask us to meet them when in India. Such meetings happen rarely, and when they do, the very same people treat us with indifference," I said.

"You can test me and see for yourself," said Dr. Mirajkar.

~

In 1939, I wanted to go to Lahore and look for stock shots on the Lahore Congress of 1929 and Lala Lajpat Rai. The proprietor of the only studio in Lahore was a Punjabi. He had studied with me in the New York Institute of Photography. (I had noted down beforehand the addresses of all my classmates from India.)

Since I was going to Lahore, I thought of Dr. Mirajkar and wrote to him mentioning the train I was taking. He received me very warmly at the railway station. He did not have a chauffeur, so he drove the car himself. We stopped in front of a huge bungalow with a sprawling garden—49 Lawrence Road, an area where the rich and the famous of Lahore lived.

After finishing my morning ablutions, I had breakfast with Dr. Mirajkar. A majestic Pathan from the Northwest Frontier waited on us.

Dr. Mirajkar said, "This is a bachelor's house—treat it like it's yours. He (the Pathan) is in charge of this house, so just let him know what you need. Since I drive my car myself, I have borrowed a car from a friend for your exclusive use as long as you are here. And you are welcome to stay here as long as you please."

He also added a warning, "You must be very careful in your business dealings—in this city they will cheat you easily. Wherever you go, say that you are my guest. It will give you some protection."

Taking leave of him I went directly to the studio. Since the proprietor had been my classmate, I had built castles in the air about an enthusiastic reception. But he treated me like any ordinary businessman.

Somehow, swallowing the disappointment, I turned my attention to the purpose of my visit.

Fortunately, whatever had been filmed during the Lahore Congress was in good condition. I selected the required portions. The next morning, I got the print after paying for it in cash. I got a receipt and also a permission letter for using it.

No stock shots of Lala Lajpat Rai could be traced.

The proprietor said, "We have footage on the Gaya Congress as well. It will take a week to trace it. After you reach Bombay, pay a hundred and fifty rupees as irrevocable deposit in a bank and send us the details. If we fail to dispatch the material within a month's time, you will get your money back."

The Gaya Congress was held in 1922 with C.R. Das as the president. We had only a single shot of C.R. Das. The Gaya Congress footage, if we got it, would be useful for linking various events and documenting the history of the Congress. The condition mentioned by the studio owner was reasonable. Since I had already bought some footage from him at a fair price, I trusted him.

On reaching Bombay, I made an irrevocable deposit of one hundred and fifty rupees in the name of the Lahore studio and informed them. After fifteen days I received a parcel from Lahore. I opened it proudly in front of Dr. Pathy and my assistant.

What a fraud! There were but a few bits of film, of one or one-and-a-half inches length.

I was thoroughly embarrassed. This was the only time I was duped (or had been gullible) in my dealings connected with the Gandhi film.

It was my punishment for not following the advice of a man of Dr. Mirajkar's experience.

A few days later I received a letter. The gist of it was: "I had the good fortune of being on the same train as the Mahatma, travelling from Delhi to Nagpur. At that time I thought of you."

The letter was from Lt. Col. Dr. Mirajkar.

As far as the film on Gandhiji was concerned, there was no end to collecting library shots; we kept collecting whatever old film that came our way.

The Dandi March or the Salt Satyagraha was a very important part of our film. We could not get any footage on it in India. We edited the two hundred feet of film we had got from different countries and included it in the documentary.

We got information that a particular individual was in possession of two rolls – approximately two thousand feet of film – on the Dandi March. We approached him at once. He was an ordinary person, not rich. Due to his reverence for Gandhiji, he had shot the Dandi March from the beginning to the end at his own expense. He had also shot the huge processions that took place in Bombay and the police lathi charge. In view of the political situation he had kept the film rolls buried in a secret place.

He said, "I spent about three thousand rupees for shooting these scenes. I am in severe financial trouble now, so pay me whatever you can."

Since we were at the final stages of production we too had financial problems. Had I the money then, I would have readily paid three thousand rupees for this rare historical treasure. But the situation was such, that there was no possibility of paying more than a thousand rupees. Further, we had to take a negative of his film and then make a copy again. Expenses were mounting.

At the same time, I did not want to exploit the poverty of a well-wisher. So I said, "We are not in a position to pay you more than one thousand rupees. We will make a copy of the thousand feet that we require and give the film back to you. This film has good potential, later people may eagerly come forward to buy it. At that point it might be possible to get back all that you had invested, or perhaps more."

He agreed to the proposal and thanked me. It was I who should have thanked him!

The film on the Dandi March was wonderful. The shooting was of a very high standard. Risking his own life, that nameless person had shot the police lathi charge at Boribandar, Bombay, in a superb manner. I was astonished at his courage and patriotism, and I paid my respects to him.

Lokmanya Bal Gangadhar Tilak had proclaimed, "Swaraj is my birthright. And I will have it." The ordeals he underwent for the country were immense. The British incarcerated Tilak, born in Ratnagiri, in Mandalay jail, Burma; and Thibaw, the king of Burma, in Ratnagiri jail. Tilak was in prison for several years.

The absence of great leaders like Dadabhai Naoroji, Lokmanya Tilak and Gopal Krishna Gokhale in our film was a source of dissatisfaction for me. But cinematography had not taken root during their time.

One day, a friend told me that someone had a film of Tilak's funeral. We went to meet this person at once. He had been in the film industry until a few years ago and had then shifted to some other profession.

When we approached him, he gave us the footage gladly. When we asked how much we should pay him, he replied, "Your undertaking is laudable—you need not pay any money."

"We are grateful for your generosity. Would it be possible for you to give us a letter to the effect that you are gifting us this film? That would be very helpful," I said. He immediately wrote the letter and gave it to us.

The box in which the film had been stored had rusted. There was a roll inside, of about four hundred feet of positive film. Since it had been shot some twenty years ago and screened in theatres hundreds of times, the sprocket perforations had widened. Therefore it could not be viewed on screen. It was certain that if we tried, the film would snap. Nor could we make a copy of it. Putting it on the printing machine for copying would only result in it snapping over and over again. A rare film in hand—but we could not use it. We felt extremely disappointed.

The next morning, Dr. Pathy and I went to the Kodak office and met a Frenchman, Quribe—an expert in cinematography. Dr. Pathy explained our problem to him.

Quribe examined the film roll for a few seconds and said, "It's very simple. Only the perforations on the upper side have widened and become weak. Turn the film upside down and make a copy. It will be a reverse print. If you print it again upside down you will get it in the right sequence."

Thus was the problem solved. By evening, we had made copies following Quribe's suggestions and screened the film for viewing. What a wonderful historical documentary! Bal Gangdhar Tilak died in the famous Sardargriha palace in Bombay, in 1920. The person who shot his final journey was none other than Dadasaheb Phalke, the father of Indian cinema. Tilak's body was clearly visible in two or three close-up shots. A documentary in 1920 India, that too, on the great Tilak—a real wonder!

A greater wonder was awaiting me in London.

There, I met Henry S.L. Polak, friend and colleague of the Mahatma. He was a Jew who ate only vegetarian food. He had participated in all the struggles in South Africa with Gandhiji and had courted arrest. On his return to England, he worked as a barrister.

I met Polak at his office. He invited me home for tea at 4 p.m. the next day. He drew a map for me as locating his house might prove to be a little difficult.

I went to his house the next evening. He introduced me to his wife. I had read about her in *My Experiments with Truth.* She, like her husband, had been a pillar of support to Gandhiji in his struggles. They received me very affectionately and plied me with tasty snacks and tea.

During the course of the evening, Henry Polak brought out an old box containing a film roll and said, "This film was shot in 1912, when Gopal Krishna Gokhale came to South Africa. It was screened in a theatre in Johannesburg meant exclusively for blacks. Afterwards, I took custody of the film. Since the film is very old, please be very careful while making the copy. Let us then view it on screen." My happiness knew no bounds.

The next morning, I took that roll to the Norman Film Library with which I was familiar. The roll was about two hundred feet long. Though the film was old, the sprocket perforations were in good condition, as it had not been screened too many times.

The person in charge told me, "We'll make the positive copy very carefully. You can come for it at four this afternon." I went there with Polak at the appointed time and the film was screened in a very special little theatre. As it had been taken in 1912, everything appeared to be happening at great speed. Gopal Krishna Gokhale came back to life and shook hands with many!

I could not see Ganshiji. I asked Polak disappointedly, "Where is the Mahatma?"

Polak pointed out, "See there, the person with Gokhale wearing western dress and Kathiawar turban, that is the Mahatma." I was utterly amazed!

This peerless film could certainly be described as one of the rare historical documents of our country. Could anybody believe that in 1912, in the African continent, which was then lagging behind in every field, someone had made a documentary, that too, on Gokhale and Gandhi? The greater wonder was that Polak had held on to it, keeping it safe, for twenty-seven years! We owe eternal gratitude to Henry Polak for having preserved this treasure and handing it over to us.

I retained one copy of the film with me and returned the original, along with another copy, to Polak. I asked him hesitantly, "How much should I pay?"

"This is my gift. It is enough if you mention that you got this from me," he said.

We encountered some difficulties in using this film. In those days, when the film was made, they shot at the speed of sixteen frames per second. Later, it became twenty-four frames per second. The content of any film will appear natural only if there are twenty-four frames per second. If the number of frames per second is less everything will appear to be taking place at very high speed.

With the help of Quribe, Dr. Pathy was able to solve this problem too. While making prints, we took the impression of the first picture once, the second picture twice, the third picture once and the fourth twice, and repeated this sequence throughout. Because of this technical alteration, the excessive speed was reduced and the action on film appeared to be taking place at a normal pace.

An excellent friend of Gandhiji had helped us by keeping this rare sequence safe for so many years!

~

When I met V.K. Krishna Menon in London, he said, "A person named Dr. Bhandari has some film shots. Meet him and say that I sent you."

Dr. Bhandari was an Indian medical practitioner. Before independence, Jawaharlal Nehru had addressed a public meeting in the famous Trafalgar Square. Dr. Bhandari had shot that event with his 16 mm camera. I got the film from him, made an enlarged copy and returned the original.

~

In 1948, when the Hindi version of our film was being produced, a Gujarati friend presented us with a film roll on the subject of the Indian National Army. There were shots of Subash Chandra Bose and of many historical incidents.

When Gandhiji died, the United Nations' flag was lowered in homage. The United Nations authorities gifted those pictures to us.

A young Gujarati from Ahmedabad, working as a junior officer in the department of agriculture, Bombay, was then living in Poona. He was a great devotee of Gandhiji. He had in his possession more than one thousand five hundred photographs and pictures of Gandhiji from newspapers. He had prepared negatives of uniform size (quarter plate), of significant photographs. I took enlargements of them and returned the negatives to him.

In South Africa, an Indian photographer provided us with enlargements of a number of photographs related to Gandhiji's association with South Africa.

We remain indebted to all those who gifted us such rare films and photographs of Gandhiji.

3

In 1939 I had the good fortune of recording on film many great men associated with Gandhiji.

Kashi is a holy place. Pandit Madan Mohan Malaviya is one of those great scholars who resided in Kashi. Everybody revered him. His service to education is unparalleled. The Banares Hindu University stands as a monument to the efforts and abilities of this individual. Even when he went to London to attend the Round Table Conference, he did not forsake his strict adherence to vedic rites—he carried with him water from the Ganga to England. He made countless sacrifices for the sake of India's independence and was one of the important senior leaders of the country.

I went to Kashi to film Malaviya in his ripe old age. We stayed in the choultry of the Nattukkottai Nagarathars who had been in the service of Kashi Viswanath for over a hundred years. Its manager, Muthu Veerappa Pillai, was an influential person. He was affectionate and helpful, and he took us around in his car to various places.

We filmed the Kashi Bharat Mata Temple, the Buddhist temples of Sarnath and the Banares Hindu University.

I met Sundaram from Tamilnadu, who was Pandit Malaviya's secretary at the Hindu University. On Malaviya's behalf, he had approached several Indian native princes and collected funds for the university. Sundaram maintained a correspondence with Gandhiji. He showed me a letter written to him by Gandhiji a few days earlier: "Last night we sang *Muthineri.*" I was thrilled to see the words 'Muthineri' written in Tamil by Gandhiji. How many among the Tamils know the meaning of 'Muthineri'?*

Sundaram took me to meet Pandit Malaviya. The elderly man was lying in bed. Getting dressed was a very difficult task for him. I said that I wanted to

---

* "Muthineri" is a poem by the Saiva poet-saint Manikkavasakar.

film only his face and therefore it would be enough if he wore his turban and coat, and that there was no need for him to wear panjakacham. Assisted by Sundaram, Malaviya came to the garden and sat on a chair. With great reverence, we shot the film.

During those few minutes in the presence of that great man, I felt overcome by emotion and a sense of awe.

Pandit Madan Mohan Malaviya, who was known as the 'Prince among Beggars', was one of those great men bound by the magic spell of Mahatma Gandhi.

~

I also had the good fortune of filming Salem C. Vijayaraghavachariar in his last days. A fearless man with sharp intellect, he scaled the peaks of the legal profession. This distinguished man had presided over the Nagpur Congress.

We filmed him with the help of his daughter Seetha Ammaiyar. Like Malaviya, he was also very old and found it difficult to tie the panjakacham. So we filmed him wearing his coat and turban.

His great height, the venerable radiance of his face with the sacred mark on the forehead remain in my memory.

~

I met the eminent Englishman Charles F. Andrews in Shantiniketan during his last days. Gandhiji called him 'Dinabandhu'.

A few days earlier, I had visited Waiz, in Bombay, with a friend. He was then the president of the Overseas Indians Association. Later, he became the commissioner of the Indian government for the Fiji Islands. He narrated an interesting anecdote about C.F. Andrews.

Andrews had stayed with Waiz for a few days in Bombay. He wanted to go to Sevagram from Bombay. Waiz gave him a hundred rupees to meet his travel expenses.

Andrews went to the railway station, where a few expatriates who had returned from British Guyana narrated their pitiable condition to him. Andrews gave them the hundred rupees and returned to Waiz's house.

Whereupon Waiz took him back to the station, bought a ticket for him, put him on a train and saw him off.

When Gandhiji came to know about this, he remarked that Andrews was but a child and it was proper that instead of giving him the money, Waiz bought him the ticket and put him on the train.

I wished to film C.F. Andrews, Gandhiji's trusted friend and the gracious god of expatriate Indians, and also record his words. Transporting the equipment from Calcutta to Shantiniketan would be expensive. So I decided to wait till he came to Calcutta.

Andrews was a living example of the maxim 'My duty is to serve ceaselessly.' When I met him, I felt as though I was in the presence of a saint. He radiated love, compassion and peace.

I spent about ten minutes with him and took a photograph of him. He told me that in a couple of months he would be in Calcutta, staying with the bishop, and that the shooting for the documentary could be done during that period.

A few days later he fell ill. He did come to Calcutta, but died within a matter of days. I was not fortunate enough to record his words on film.

The photograph I had taken of him in Shantiniketan turned out to be splendid.

~

I wanted to record Sir C.V. Raman's opinion of Gandhiji on film.

The Nobel laureate was then in Bangalore. When I wrote to him, he replied giving me the date of his visit to Chennai and suggested that the shooting could be done on that day. I made arrangements for the shooting at Newtone Studio.

On the day of the shooting I had to be in Bombay due to some unexpected work. I had to entrust the shooting to our office manager. Sir C.V. Raman did not refer to Gandhiji as the Mahatma. Since I wanted him to use the reverential term, I left instructions with our office manager. "Sir C.V. Raman does not normally use the term 'Mahatma'. When the shooting is about to start, greet him and request him to say 'Mahatma'. Don't give him time to think."

I came to know later that everything had proceeded as per my wishes. Sir C.V. Raman had uttered 'Mahatma' with stress and clarity, and had spoken a few sentences wholeheartedly praising Gandhiji's anti-untouchability campaign.

I regretted not having been present on that occasion, though I was happy that his words had been recorded for the film.

A few years later, during the Asian Relations Conference in New Delhi, I was waiting in the reception room. But for a Punjabi woman working there, nobody else was present. A car appeared suddenly. Sir C.V. Raman got out of the car, went straight up to the woman and asked for some information. She did not know that he was Raman. I introduced myself to him and told him about the Gandhi film and the recording of his speech for it. He nodded his head and put some questions to the woman. Thereupon he was lost in thought for a while and left abruptly.

After he left, I told the woman, "That was Sir C.V. Raman."

The woman was surprised, "What? He disappeared without saying anything."

I said, "That's C.V. Raman."

~

A few years after that, I was staying in the house of my friend Pratap Asher, in Tiruppur. The meetings of the Tiruppur Rotary Club were held there every week.

During one of the meetings Pratap arranged for us to listen to Sir C.V. Raman's speech recorded during the Bangalore Rotary Conference. We listened to it eagerly. The following sentences, spoken in English, are even now deeply etched in my mind:

> I attended a conference in Argentina. A man came to me and said, "I am a scientist from Norway." I told him, "I do not care whether you are from Norway or Timbuktu. You are a scientist. That is enough for me."

~

In 1937, I was staying in an international youth hostel called International House, in New York. There were hundreds of students from various countries residing in that hostel and studying in different colleges.

One day, at about ten in the night a woman student working in the reception hall told me, "There is a call from the *New York Times.* They want to talk to an Indian student. Could you please take that call?"

Among the twelve Indian students staying in the hostel, I was the only one present. I was still new to the place and everybody else had gone out.

"We are from the *New York Times.* How do you pronounce the name 'Rajagopalachariar', and what is the spelling?" Since I was from Chennai I was able to give them the correct answers. They thanked me for my help.

The next morning, there was a small editorial on Rajaji in the *New York Times.* In America too there is a town called Salem. Though the spelling is the same the pronunciation is different. The prohibition of liquor imposed in the American Salem had been an utter failure. The editorial mentioned that Rajaji, the premier of the Madras State, had implemented prohibition in his hometown Salem successfully.

I cut out that article and dispatched it to Rajaji by airmail. He wrote from the Thiruchengode Ashram thanking me for the clipping.

Towards the end of 1938, Gandhiji was staying in a Harijan settlement called Bhangi Colony in New Delhi. The executive committee meeting of the Congress was held there. Several senior leaders, including Rajaji, were staying in that colony. I was in Delhi at that time on a visit. Sardar Vedaratnam Pillai of Vedaranyam introduced me to Rajaji.

I requested a favour from Rajaji. "We wish to make a documentary on prohibition in Salem. Please help us by giving instructions to the collector of Salem district."

"There is complete prohibition in Salem now. So how will you manage to make a documentary of that?" countered Rajaji.

"We will film the toddy shops in the adjacent district of Coimbatore and contrast it with the situation in Salem where prohibition is in force," I replied.

Rajaji nodded his head, but firmly refused to extend any help.

When I went to Salem to film C. Vijayaraghavachariar, I planned to also film the toddy shops that had been converted into tea shops after the prohibition. Pandaram, the manager of the khadi shop there, was an ardent patriot. He received us very affectionately and accompanied us when we went on two horse-drawn carts to an erstwhile toddy shop. Our presence angered the shop owner. Already sore over the loss of income because of prohibition, he became furious on seeing us shooting his shop. After a few minutes, two or three stones were thrown at us—and then came a volley. We called an end to the shooting and left immediately.

~

The Congress contested for the first time during the 1937 assembly elections and captured seven out of the eleven provinces and formed ministries in Bombay, Madras, the United Provinces, the Central Provinces, Orissa, Assam and the North-West Frontier Province.

In our film, we followed the method of showing the portraits of the premiers and mentioning the provinces, but not their names. The available pictures were very old, so we thought of photographing them afresh.

I made arrangements for taking photographs of Rajaji in Chennai. Kalki R. Krishnamurthy took me to Rajaji's house, introduced me to him, described the Gandhi film in detail and mentioned the purpose of my visit.

Rajaji said, "You Chettiars have established yourselves in the film industry. Are you now producing this documentary on Gandhi because there is no money in feature films?"

I remained silent.

Kalki argued with Rajaji earnestly and tried to convince him that mine was not a commercial but a patriotic venture. He assured Rajaji that there was no need for apprehension, as he was fully aware of everything about the film. But Rajaji, who never trusted anybody, refused to cooperate.

We requested Rajaji to come out to be photographed. "Please come to the garden. The photograph will be good only if there is enough light."

"No, I cannot come out. Photograph me where I am."

There wasn't sufficient light in the small hall where Rajaji was sitting. We had no other choice but to photograph him there. The result was not good.

We could never forget Kalki's unsolicited help, his concern for the film and finally his excellent review of it after the release.

~

The Sabarmati is one of the holy rivers of India. After returning from South Africa, Gandhiji started an ashram near Ahmedabad on the banks of the Sabarmati. The Sabarmati Ashram was a monument for simplicity, truth, discipline, purity, sacrifice and integrity. Gandhiji set off on the Dandi Salt March from the Ashram in 1930. We went to Ahmedabad to shoot that holy place.

Narhari Parikh, a Gandhi devotee, was the manager of the ashram. He was one of those who considered themselves the chosen heirs of Gandhiji. I met him and asked for permission to shoot the Ashram.

"How much money will you give?" he asked.

"This is a film about the country's independence. It is doubtful whether the film will be completed and even if it is completed whether it will be screened. We have earmarked ten per cent of the net profits for institutions connected with Gandhiji," I replied.

He insisted that twenty-five per cent must be given to the Sabarmati Ashram.

We returned, unable to do the shooting. I thought of Mridulabehn Sarabhai, the daughter of Ambalal Sarabhai. Though a millionaire and the chairman of many mills, Ambalal Sarabhai was a Gandhian.

Mridula Behn received us cordially. She was immensely happy to know that we were producing a documentary on Gandhiji. She immediately wrote a letter to Narhari Parikh in Gujarati, and gave it to us, "Take this letter to him. He will permit you to do the shooting."

We went to the Ashram again. Parikh was away. His assistant read the letter and said, "You can shoot as you please. I will assist you in all possible ways." We stayed there for about an hour and completed the shooting.

~

In Allahabad, the office of the All India Congress Committee was housed in Anand Bhavan, a large mansion donated to the country by the Nehru family. After the transfer of ownership its name was changed to Swaraj Bhavan. The Nehrus built a small bungalow for themselves nearby and named it Anand Bhavan.

We planned to film Swaraj Bhavan and Jawaharlal Nehru.

Once I happened to travel on the same train as Acharya Kripalani who was returning to Allahabad from Bombay. I travelled by the old second class. In those days railway coupons could be bought at twenty per cent discount by making advance payment. There were many private railway companies and the coupons were valid everywhere, except in the case of the Bengal–Nagpur or B.N. Railway.

Second class travel was very comfortable. Generally, there were four berths in a two-tiered compartment, with toilet facilities for each compartment. Since there were only a few passengers, seats were available freely. Sometimes I had been the only passenger for hours together. During long journeys I bathed in the compartment and changed into fresh clothes. In Switzerland, I had once bought a sleek and beautiful typewriter, weighing seven pounds, for fifty-two rupees. It had travelled thousands of miles with me.

On the appointed day I went to the Victoria Terminus, Bombay, at ten in the night. Acharya Kripalani was standing on the platform with about fifteen people who had come to see him off.

Kripalani was travelling by interclass, a nondescript class between the comfortable second and the uncomfortable third. It would be a compartment either partitioned into small sections, or large and undivided, with a capacity of sixty-four seats. Acharya Kripalani's compartment was not partitioned and was excessively crowded.

The next morning, when the train halted at a station, I got down from my compartment to go and see him. All the other passengers had vacated the interclass compartment. He was alone in that large compartment. I got in and greeted him.

Kriplani enquired kindly whether I had boarded the train at that station. "No. I am coming from Bombay. I saw you in the station yesterday," I said.

He remarked in English, "You look so fresh!"

I told him briefly about the Gandhi film. He listened to me with keen interest. I told him about what Narhari Parikh had demanded for shooting in the Sabarmati Ashram.

"Narhari wants a share in your profits. But if you incur loss, will he share that too?" asked Kripalani.

I did not attempt an answer.

Kripalani reassured me, "You are doing what we should be doing! It is our duty to help you in all possible ways. Come to Allahabad, I will throw open the whole Congress building. You can shoot what you want."

Acharya Kripalani belonged to the Sindh Province. When Gandhiji started his satyagraha in Champaran in Bihar, Kripalani, who was then a college professor, got in touch with Gandhiji and joined the venerable galaxy of patriots.

He possessed a keen intellect and a fine sense of humour. He never hankered for office but observed the ideal 'My duty is to serve.' He had the spirit of independence to stand against anybody, except Gandhiji. He had gone to jail several times and had been the secretary of the All India Congress for many years, and its president for a short period. He was very amiable and would be friendly with everybody, like a child.

Acharya Kripalani shared some of his reminiscences with me. The two-hour conversation with this great leader was one of the fortunate occasions of my life.

~

We went to Allahabad and met Acharya Kripalani at the Congress secretariat. He instructed Sadiq Ali, the executive secretary, to do the needful. We filmed everything—the places, the deed donating the Nehru family mansion to our country, Acharya Kripalani spinning with a charka.

"Jawaharlal Nehru is coming here tomorrow, but I am leaving for Calcutta. Please help us so that my team can film him," I requested Kripalani. He gladly agreed.

It was only later that I got to know how Dr. Pathy completed the shooting.

The next day, Dr. Pathy went with Acharya Kripalani and met Nehru in Anand Bhavan. At that time, Nehru was taking a stroll in the front veranda of the upper storey of the building. Since Acharya Kripalani made the introduction Nehru consented to being filmed. He had then asked Dr. Pathy, "How should I pose?" Dr. Pathy had replied that he could do as he wished. On hearing this, Nehru turned his back to the camera. Without a word Dr. Pathy began filming him from behind! Nehru then turned around and smiled. In the film, we used only the smiling Nehru.

When Dr. Pathy expressed his desire to film Nehru while he was spinning, Nehru said, "I can't spin for you to capture me on film! You have to shoot the film when I spin!"

Dr. Pathy asked with trepidation, "At what time will you do that?"

"Afternoon, four o'clock," pat came the reply.

Dr. Pathy went to Anand Bhavan at a quarter to four. The servants told him that Nehru was asleep. Nobody had the temerity to wake him. But exactly at four Nehru came out of his room with a box charka and sat down to spin. Dr. Syed Ahmad who had come to see him sat in a chair nearby.

Some people are born photogenic—they look even better in their photographs than they do in real life. John Gunther, a famous American writer, had written that Nehru was one such person. It is absolutely true.

With the thread spun by Nehru one could weave only a rug, not a vetti. The thread would snap often and he would set it right. Dr. Pathy continued filming even when the thread snapped. Nehru would then scowl at the camera. Whenever this scene appeared on the screen the audience laughed delightedly.

It cannot be said with certainty that Nehru had faith in khadi. Nehru did the spinning only because it was a mark of discipline required from a freedom fighter.

Nobody, except Gandhiji, could have made Nehru spin the charka.

~

The year 1938. Gandhi was living in Sevagram near Wardha. For the shooting of our film, we went and stayed in Wardha several times. From there we would go to Sevagram everyday. Dr. Pathy and two of his assistants did the shooting very ably.

One day, when we went to the office of Mahadev Desai, Pyarelal was with him. I heard Desai tell Pyarelal, "Tomorrow morning Dr. Radhakrishnan is coming to meet Bapuji. Since he is travelling such a long distance to come here, set apart at least an hour for him." At that time, Radhakrishnan was a professor of Indian Philosophy at the University of Oxford. He had come home on vacation.

The next morning, Radhakrishnan came to Sevagram in his usual coat and turban. I saw him for the first time.

We wanted to include the opinions of great men who were contemporaries of Gandhiji in our film. Prominent in that list were Sir Radhakrishnan and Sir C.V. Raman.

When Radhakrishnan was the vice-chancellor of the University of Calcutta we wrote to him expressing our wish. I made a trip to Calcutta exclusively for this purpose. I went to Radhakrishnan's house and said that we wanted him to speak just three lines about Gandhiji for our film. He agreed gladly. He asked us to come at 8.30 in the morning and take him to the studio, and then to drop him off at the university before 10 o'clock.

I went to the office of Aurora Film Corporation at Dharamtollah and met its proprietor Anathi Bose. Bose is one of the pioneers of Bengali cinema. He owned a studio in Calcutta with a branch office in Chennai. He had a special affection for people from Chennai. It was he who made the documentary on the Chennai Congress presided by Dr. Ansari. Besides, he had also filmed occasions such as the Calcutta Congress and the inaugural function of Shantiniketan. He opened up his treasurehouse of films and said that I could take whatever I liked. From the beginning he treated me like his younger brother. He was never businesslike in his interaction with me. He would say, "Making the Gandhi film is a good deed. Take all that you need. Pay me what you like, what you can."

Calcutta is famous for rasgollas, and I am very fond of them. Anathi Bose would offer me huge quantities of rasgollas, sandesh and other Bengali sweets. I would struggle to eat it all.

I could take liberties with him, therefore I said, "Tomorrow I am bringing Radhakrishnan to the studio. I intend to record his speech on Gandhiji for my film. You know the type of people who come to cinema studios—rarely do great men visit studios. Shouldn't we make an attempt to clean it up?"

"You need not have any anxiety on that score. I'll go there myself and supervise the work. Just bring him there on time," said Anathi Bose.

I went to meet the famous director M.L. Tandon at his house in Calcutta. Tandon was from the Punjab. When he was very poor, one of his relatives took him to Canada. Tandon did manual work in orchards in the Vancouver area and earned enough to join a cinema course taught by the famous Russian, Professor Morgovin, at the University of Southern California, Los Angeles. Once when I met Professor Morgovin, he spoke to me with pride about his student Tandon. For a while Tandon worked in Hollywood studios. After returning to India he lived in Chennai for a few years. Tandon was a large man who wore heavy spectacles; he was very generous and had a fine sense of humour. He was an expert editor, especially good in the technique of inter-cutting.

As usual, Tandon welcomed me affectionately. I asked for his suggestions regarding the shooting. He said, "Radhakrishnan is a great man. Don't use a hired car, take my car. I'll come to the studio tomorrow morning and supervise everything. Don't worry."

The next morning, I reached Radhakrishnan's house before the appointed time in Tandon's large, comfortable car (imported from America). He was ready and waiting.

What a surprise when we reached the studio! They had cleaned the studio and had beautified the entrance with rangoli and decorated it with festoons. Beauty and harmony reigned where there had been vulgarity and cacophony. Anathi Bose and Tandon welcomed Radhakrishnan at the gate. I introduced them to Radhakrishnan. They took him inside. All the employees paid their respects.

Since the preparations had already been made, the shooting started immediately under Tandon's supervision. Radhakrishnan took out a piece of paper from his pocket and read out the three sentences he had written especially for the occasion:

> Gandhi's supreme faith in God and non-violence makes him a profoundly religious man.

> It is his devotion to religion that has compelled him into politics and so his political creed does no injury to the spiritual tradition of the country.
>
> If he appeals to the British people, it is not as an agitator or a revolutionary, but as a servant of humanity, interested in the reconciliation of mankind.

Radhakrishnan's speech was published in the *Hindu* the next day.

The shooting was over in fifteen minutes. Tandon said to me, "Escort him to the university and come back. I'll wait for you."

Radhakrishnan was given a warm send-off. He got down outside the university gate and said to me in English, "Normally people in the cinema field do not keep their word. You have brought me here well before the time agreed upon."

I respectfully took leave.

Anathi Bose was extremely happy about Radhakrishnan's visit to his studio. I got another helping of rasgollas!

Whenever I think of Calcutta, Anathi Bose comes to my mind.

~

The film depicting the life of Gandhiji, with commentary in Tamil, was screened on 23 August 1940. A few months later, the film was screened with Telugu commentary. But the turbulent political situation and the fear that the government might confiscate the film stopped us from screening it any further in public.

In the later half of 1942, Radhakrishnan came to Chennai and stayed in his house on Edward Elliot's Road. He had not yet seen the film. I wished to screen it for him and his family. Radhakrishnan happily agreed to come for the special screening.

I made arrangements in a small theatre in Gemini Studio.

I approached a press baron in Chennai and requested him to lend one of his cars, as it would not be proper to offer Radhakrishnan hired transport. He gave me the most comfortable car he had. Radhakrishnan saw the big car and with a smile remarked in English, "Knowing my difficulties you have brought a big car." We reached Gemini Studio on time.

I had also invited five or six well-wishers to see the film along with Radhakrishnan. One of them was T.T. Krishnamachari.

In the film, Radhakrishnan appeared in the All Party Conference held in Calcutta in 1928. The scene shot in Calcutta with his speech was also there. He looked pleased.

After the screening was over, he exchanged a few words with the other invitees. I accompanied him and his family back home, and took leave.

In 1952–53, we made an agreement with a trust called the American Academy of Asian Studies, San Francisco, for releasing the English version of the Gandhi film. I mentioned this to Radhakrishnan.

I was staying in the YMCA building in San Francisco. At midnight I was told that a special messenger had come from the secretariat of the Indian ambassador to personally deliver a letter to me.

The letter was from Radhakrishnan. He was then the vice president of India. Letters written by the president, the vice president, the prime minister and such dignitaries were sent in special diplomatic bags, by air, once or twice a week. Special messengers delivered the letters immediately on arrival. Though the address given in the letter was different, the consulate knew where I was staying.

> Dr. S. Radhakrishnan
>
> Council of State Secretariat
> Parliament House
> New Delhi
> 14 May 1952
>
> My dear Chettiar,
>
> It is good to hear from you.
>
> I am glad to know that you are enlisting the support of the American Academy of Asian Studies for your documentary film on Gandhi.
>
> Yours sincerely,
> S. Radhakrishnan

Shri A.K. Chettiar
Care Vedanta Society
Hindu Temple
2963 Webster Street
San Francisco, 23, California

Generally, Radhakrishnan's letters were brief and kind. He wrote the addressee's name in his own hand and made corrections. The receiver would get the impression that Radhakrishnan had gone through the whole letter before despatching it. This was a special feature of his letters.

~

The film director, K. Subrahmanyam, came to America with a film delegation in 1952. I met him in Los Angeles. We stayed together for a few days. He insisted that I write a letter to the films division of the United Nations. The name of a very important person had to be cited as reference in that letter. I wrote to Radhakrishnan asking for his permission to use his name. The reply, "You can use my name as reference," came at once.

~

In 1964, I had to go to New Delhi to attend to some work for a friend. At that time Radhakrishnan was the president of India. I wrote to his secretary expressing my wish to meet and pay my respects to the president, and that the reply could be sent to my friend's address in New Delhi.

As soon as I reached New Delhi, I met my friend, who joyfully informed me that an invitation had come from the Rashtrapathi Bhavan. But he had misplaced the invitation. He had then contacted the Rashtrapathi Bhavan, told them that the invitation got lost on its way to Chennai by post, and noted down the date and time of appointment.

I went there fifteen minutes ahead of the appointed time. Usually those who came to meet the president had to carry the cards issued to them. Since information had already been given about the loss of my card, there was no hitch in gaining entry.

Krishnamurthy, one of the president's secretaries, came to the reception hall where I had been asked to wait. I was acquainted with him.

After conversing with me for a while, he asked me when I had met the president first. I told him about the shooting done in the year 1939 for the Gandhi film. He then took leave of me.

At the appointed time, a man in military uniform came to receive me. He opened a door to a passage that was about twenty feet long. At the end of the passage there was another door. Before opening this door he asked me, "Do you know the president?" I said, "Yes." If not, the custom was to announce the name of the president first and then the name of the guest. I knew this as I had earlier visited Rajaji.

The room was called the president's chamber, but it was actually a very big hall. The president was sitting in a corner. The military officer ushered me in.

I went up to the place where Radhakrishnan was sitting. He stood up, held my hands affectionately and made me sit near him.

His first question was, "Is Rajaji in good health?"

Then he enquired about *Kumari Malar* and said that he had seen its office on Mowbray's Road. I felt thrilled to hear this.

Mixing Tamil and English, he said, "Have I forgotten your coming to my small house in Calcutta in 1939 and shooting that film?"

I was astonished that he could still recall that incident.

I said, "After my meeting with you, I went to Europe and met Romain Rolland and did some shooting for the film. He asked me what I intended to do next. I told him that I was going to London to film Bernard Shaw. He said, 'Bernard Shaw is an eccentric. He might say something in commendation of Gandhi, or something mischievous. If he says anything mischievous, you will not include it in the film. Immediately he may issue a press note. So, do not go to him.' I took his advice."

Radhakrishnan replied in English, "I think you did a wise thing in following Romain Rolland's advice. I had a similar experience. I wrote to Shaw asking for an article to be included in the volume honouring Gandhiji's seventieth birthday. You know what Shaw wrote to me? 'Gandhi never cared to write about me when I reached seventy. Why should I write about him?' "

That was my last meeting with Radhakrishnan.

I took leave of him.

4

I have referred to the Mahatma's dominating personality, and we must admit how difficult it is to shake off his spell even for those individuals that desired to do so. I feel certain that Mahatma Gandhi neither asked, nor wanted anyone to surrender his judgment to him; and I have been told that just before his arrest he regretfully realised that quite a number of his followers and admirers, who had readily, and in all sincerity, signified their agreement with him failed to realize that they were offering their allegiance only to the man and were not accepting his measures as well on the strength of their own clear conviction.

Presidential address by Maulana Mohammed Ali
Kakinada Congress, 1923

He is undoubtedly one of the greatest men that the world has ever seen. ... he will be gratefully remembered, now and always, by a nation that he led from victory to victory.

Presidential address by Deshbandhu C.R. Das
Gaya Congress, 1922

The most blessed days of my life were those that I spent in Sevagram filming Gandhiji's life!

In 1939, Gandhiji stayed in a Harijan settlement called the Bhangi Colony in New Delhi. Most of the leaders of the country were there. Sardar Vedaratnam Pillai introduced me to Seth Jamnalal Bajaj.

Jamnalal Bajaj was a millionaire. Gandhiji had four sons, and he considered Jamnalal his fifth. Jamnalal perceived himself as only the trustee of his limitless properties and lived accordingly. He was a model of love, modesty, simplicity and sacrifice. Jamnalal Bajaj, the karmayogi, lived in Wardha. His devoted wife matched her exemplary husband in every aspect.

In 1930, while setting off to Dandi for the Salt Satyagraha, Gandhiji undertook a vow that he would return to the Sabarmati Ashram only after swaraj was achieved.

As soon as Gandhiji was released from jail, Jamnalal Bajaj requested him to come and stay in the small ashram he was planning to set up in Wardha. Gandhiji agreed to his request.

Wardha is a town located right at the centre of India. The distance between Nagpur, the capital of the Central Provinces, and Wardha was almost forty miles. Wardha was situated near the rail track to Delhi. Most of the town belonged to Jamnalal. He built a very simple ashram, that came to be known as the Sevagram, three miles from Wardha.

Countless people who came from various parts of the world to seek Gandhiji's blessings or to converse with him stayed in the guesthouse in Sevagram. There was an old model Ford car in the guesthouse. The path to Sevagram was very bumpy and the car was suitable for that track. Gandhiji would travel between Sevagram and Wardha by that car.

Nobody would enter the cottage in which Gandhiji stayed without permission. People from all over the world came to Sevagram and stayed there to seek his blessings in the mornings and evenings when he came out for his walk. It became a place of pilgrimage as the spirit of nationalism rose in India.

The image of a hand charka was etched on the mud wall of his cottage. There was a garden in the front. The cottage was surrounded by a fence to prevent cattle from straying in.

People said there was no lock for his room. In fact, there was not even a door. Gandhiji was one of the holy saints of India who, having nothing to hide, lived a truly open life!

There were many small buildings with tiled roofs in Sevagram. Mother Kasturba stayed in one such building. The inmates of the ashram lived in another such building. Aryanayakam, who had formulated and then implemented Basic Education,* lived in another small building with his wife Asha Devi.

---

* A radical scheme of education formulated by Gandhi in 1937 which envisaged seven years of compulsory, free education for all children: knowledge would be

A building was set apart for guests. J.C. Kumarappa, the secretary of the All India Village Industries Association, and his younger brother, Bharatan Kumarappa, stayed in a nearby building. There were a few more buildings in the ashram. All the buildings were located well apart from one another. Sevagram exemplified the Indian rural environment.

~

We set off for Wardha from Bombay. There was a long building partitioned into four rooms and let out to travellers near the Wardha railway station. We rented two of the rooms. There was a vast open space in the front with a number of trees. We hired a car at Rs 10 per day; we had to pay for the petrol ourselves. We did no other work than shooting for the film at Sevagram.

Some of the people who went to Sevagram from Wardha, to seek the blessings of Gandhiji, walked and some others went by tongas—small horse-drawn carriages. Only important guests would be given the guesthouse car. Some would ask us for the car we had hired. If they were important people, we would take them with us to Sevagram. Otherwise we would lend the car free of rent.

I still remember the first day of shooting. We were shooting Gandhiji's cottage from a distance and Gandhiji's grandson (Ramdas Gandhi's son who was about six years old) was with us, watching the shooting. Maulana Abul Kalam Azad appeared all of a sudden. Immediately, Dr. Pathy turned the camera to film Abul Kalam Azad walking towards Gandhiji's cottage. While turning around with his camera, he stamped on the little boy's foot. The boy started crying loudly. On hearing his screams, Mother Kasturba who was in the nearby building rushed out. Jamnalal Bajaj's daughter too rushed out. Abul Kalam Azad walked back to pacify the boy. We did not know what to do. We feared that we might have to stop the shooting.

---

imparted through manual training rather than from books; the mother tongue would be the medium of instruction; and the entire scheme was to be financed by the labour of the pupils.

At this point, Jamnalal Bajaj's daughter began to sing a Hindi song. On hearing her, the boy stopped crying at once and smiled. I understood the magic of that song later.

The song meant, "Whatever misery may befall me, I will bear it with joy."

~

I met the world famous Japanese poet Yone Noguchi in Japan, in 1936. He had recently returned from a trip to India and narrated his travel experiences. He said, "I paid my reverential respects to the Mahatma. His secretary Mahadev Desai is an epitome of modesty."

Mahadev Desai was remarkable for his humility, kindness, generosity, discipline and efficiency. He served Gandhiji for more than twenty-five years. For him, this opportunity was a gift from God. After Gandhiji returned from South Africa and began his public life, Mahadev Desai, a man of absolute integrity, served as his most trusted secretary everyday, inside and outside prison. There was none who knew the mind of Gandhiji as Desai did.

I met Desai and paid my respects soon after I reached Sevagram. His advice was, "Do the shooting as you would like to. But don't trouble anybody."

Desai would not talk much, and never unnecessarily. Whatever happened in any corner of the far-flung Sevagram, it would come to the immediate notice of Desai. He was keen on doing his duty without any fuss. His was a childlike nature.

Desai would be present with Gandhiji whenever important people came to visit him. He would take down the gist of the conversation faithfully.

It is said that Mahadev Desai's style of writing English was exactly like Gandhiji's. Desai translated into English Gandhiji's autobiography and several other books written in Gujarati, his mother tongue.

It was Gandhiji's good fortune that Desai happened to be his personal assistant.

~

A woman from Punjab had dedicated both her children to the noble service of Gandhiji—Pyarelal and his younger sister, Dr. Sushila Nayyar.

Pyarelal was then a young man. He was brisk and active by nature, and he assisted Mahadev Desai.

Sushila Nayyar was a physician. She took care of the small dispensary in the ashram. She, who was blessed with the opportunity of treating Gandhiji, later became free India's minister for health.

Pyarelal's *The Last Phase,* written after Gandhiji's death, is one of the finest Gandhian books.

~

Aryanayakam – who ably assisted Gandhiji in formulating Basic Education and later dedicated his whole life to the execution of this project – and his very knowledgeable wife, Asha Devi, lived in Sevagram.

Aryanayakam was a Tamil from Jaffna. He had studied in Russia for a few years, and had lived and worked with Rabindranath Tagore in Shantiniketan for many years. He had married Asha Devi of Bengal.

Aryanayakam was one of the many erudite scholars bound by the magic spell of Gandhiji. He had adopted a very simple life which exemplifed the motto, 'My only duty is to serve.'

Aryanayakam was six feet tall; he had an impressive physique and a kind disposition. His wife Asha Devi's hospitality was remarkable.

Everyone in Sevagram had to lead austere lives. Shelter was provided. Those staying with families were allotted a small garden for growing vegetables. Each person had to spin and weave the cloth necessary for them. Everyone was given Rs 15 a month for meeting personal expenses.

Coffee was hard to come by in Sevagram. If we wanted coffee we would seek refuge in Aryanayakam's house. There, we were certain to get good, hot coffee.

Aryanayakam spoke very good Tamil—but Jaffna Tamil. In a letter to a friend he wrote that he would try to meet him during his forthcoming visit to Chennai. But the Jaffna Tamil word he had used to mean 'would try' (*thendippaen)* caused confusion and amusement. The friend showed the letter to me and asked, "What crime did I commit? Why does he want to punish me?" (For the people of Tamilnadu 'thendippaen' means "I will punish you.")

When Aryanayakam inaugurated the training school for Basic Education at Ramakrishna Vidyalaya, Coimbatore, I had the opportunity to listen to his wonderful Tamil speech.

Aryanayakam and his wife were learned scholars. They had the potential to earn money in a big way. It was Gandhiji who inspired them to dedicate themselves to the service of humankind.

~

The All India Village Industries Association was located in Maganwadi near Sevagram. The place was named Maganwadi in memory of Maganlal, Gandhiji's nephew, who had died young. He had been in South Africa with Gandhiji and had participated in all the struggles and courted arrest. On his return to India he had stayed with Gandhiji and served the community until his death.

Gandhiji was the president of the All India Village Industries Association. J.C. Kumarappa was the secretary. A native of Tirunelveli, he had studied in an American university for his doctorate in economics. After returning from America, he met Gandhiji at the Sabarmati Ashram. Gandhiji was sitting on the floor. Since Kumarappa was in western dress, Gandhiji asked for a chair to be brought. They both conversed for a very long time. The result was Kumarappa was won over by Gandhijis ideas on economics. He opted for a simple life and became one of the foremost among the holy group of patriots who dedicated their knowledge, talents and lives to the welfare of the nation.

Many village handicraft industries like papermaking and jaggery production developed in Maganwadi. We filmed the English woman, Muriel Lester, smilingly operate a small stone hand-mill. When Gandhiji went to London to participate in the Round Table Conference, it was Muriel Lester who had been his host at Kingsley Hall, situated in east London, an area inhabited by poor people.

Gandhiji inaugurated the museum that was established in Maganwadi. When a four-year-old girl garlanded him, he took off the garland at once and put it around the child's neck. Then suddenly, to everybody's surprise, he inserted his head into the garland and began to affectionately play with the child. The photograph depicting this scene is one of those rare pictures that capture the warmth and humanity in Gandhiji's personality.

Since the inauguration took place in the evening, the light was not sufficient for filming. So Dr. Pathy employed the slow motion technique. The result was excellent and innumerable people enjoyed seeing it. We owe this splendid shot to Dr. Pathy's presence of mind.

Let me narrate another incident. When Gandhiji was travelling as a third-class passenger on the *Rajputana* to participate in the Second Round Table Conference as India's sole representative, he tended a fellow passenger's child lovingly. We included in the film a shot that had captured the pretty little child laughing happily with her mouth open, with a matching laugh from Gandhiji's toothless mouth. In the film, these two delightful scenes of Gandhiji with the children elicited thunderous applause from lakhs and lakhs of people.

~

When I went to South Africa to shoot for the film, I met Mrs. P.K. Naidu and Mrs. Thambi Naidu in Johannesburg on different occasions. These two women and their late husbands had been in the forefront of Gandhiji's struggle and had been jailed for their activities. Gandhiji had written in praise of them in his *Satyagraha in South Africa*.

I filmed both these ladies. Both gave me letters written to Gandhiji with a request that I must personally deliver them to him.

I took these letters to Sevagram—letters written by two women who had participated and courted arrest with Gandhiji in the South African satyagraha, and who were now living thousands of miles away and had not met him for several years. Delivering the letters personally to Gandhiji would have provided me a chance to exchange a few words with him. Who could resist the desire to meet him, even if it were for just a single word?

But I did not meet Gandhiji. I posted the letters and ensured that they reached Sevagram. Let not anybody think I missed the rare chance of meeting Gandhiji that came my way accidentally, or that I sacrificed my desire to speak with him. I did not utilise the opportunity because my desire to complete the film was stronger than my desire to meet him.

If I were to meet him, Gandhiji might ask me what I was doing. Then I would have to say, "Bapuji, I am producing a documentary on you." Gandhiji might say, "Don't do that." And that would be the final word!

I prayed to God that such a situation should not arise due to any reason.

My prayers bore fruit.

❧

One morning, about fifty Hindustan scouts cleaned a whole village near Sevagram. Gandhiji attended the evening meeting. The scouts stood in a circle. Gandhiji hoisted their flag, and asked them to sit around him and advised them. We got the opportunity to film this programme.

Gandhiji would go for walks in the mornings and evenings. He would walk very fast. Those who walked with him had to run at times to keep up with him. While walking, Gandhiji would greet whomsoever he came across with folded hands.

Among those who went for walks with him, there was the very tall American, Dr. Peter Booke. He was an expert in naturopathy. He was interested in Hinduism and he followed Gandhian principles. Besides taking photographs of Gandhiji, he also made a short film.

People of all ranks – from kings to beggars – came to seek Gandhiji's blessings. Among them was Appa Saheb Pant, the prince of Awadh. He had studied in England for many years. His father, the Maharaja of Awadh, was known for his worship of the sun. Not only did he worship the sun everyday, but he also promoted the benefits of sun worship.

Awadh was a small native state. The princes of many such small states were servile towards the British, and in turn treated their subjects as slaves. Generally, the plight of the people living in these native states was more miserable than their counterparts living in British India. While their people were sinking in poverty, the princes were squandering public wealth, indulging in alcohol and undesirable entertainment in foreign countries.

There was a Resident of the British government for every state. The Resident's word was law.

In such a situation, the ruler of Awadh came forward to offer responsible government to the people of his state. He requested Gandhiji to draft the constitution. It was the first constitution drafted by Gandhiji.

~

I wished to make a short film, in colour, of Gandhiji in the natural and rural atmosphere of Sevagram, as a keepsake. Colour film was still at trial stage then. Yet, many different kinds of colour film had begun to appear in the market. One among them was Dufay, manufactured in England. The cost of a hundred feet of colour film was Rs 80, whereas ordinary film of the same length cost only Rs 14. For developing the colour film, the negatives had to be sent to London. The cost of the film was inclusive of the developing charge, but not the postal expense.

We used a hundred feet of colour film and sent it to London. The developed print reached us after two months. It was no good. Apart from the loss of money, we experienced disappointment.

As far as I knew, nobody had shot a 35-mm colour film of Gandhiji. A few might have done it with 16-mm film, in a small way. Once, in New Delhi, I came across a short kodochrome colour film of Gandhiji. My amiable friend, Sud, an expert photographer and the proprietor of Delhi Photo Studios, had shot the film. It was taken while Gandhiji was returning from the viceroy's palace in New Delhi. The palace, surrounded by a garden in full bloom, formed the background. There was optimum sunlight. Gandhiji walking in his usual swift stride with his retinue and Sarojini Devi clad in a colourful sari provided a marvellous feast for the viewers' eyes.

~

I encountered some eccentric people in Sevagram. The principal of the Basic Training School in Wardha was a young Muslim. He had a strange request for me, "Take a photograph of me with Gandhiji. I'll give you ten rupees."

There was a Buddhist monk from Japan in Sevagram. He went about, like a mendicant, beating a round bronze plate with a small stick. I wanted to photograph him. But he hid his face with the plate. I requested him earnestly with the few Japanese words I knew. It was of no avail. I thought he was one among those rare few who did not like being filmed.

In ten minutes the same monk returned after having had a wash and a change of clothes, and requested us with a smile to film him.

~

Once Dr. Pathy went to Sevagram alone. There he met a young man named Raghubir Singh who had studied in England for four years and had married an English girl. Raghubir's father was a judge in the Allahabad High Court. Raghubir had undergone a course in cinematography. He wanted to stay in Sevagram as our agent and do the shooting for our film.

On the recommendation of Dr. Pathy, we appointed Raghubir Singh as our operative cameraman and paid him Rs 100 per month. We paid him third-class railway fare or bus fare for his travels and sent him a small DeVry camera by post.

Disaster struck on the very first day. Raghubir filmed Gandhiji while he was returning from his bath. Gandhiji would stare angrily at anybody who filmed him while he was eating or bathing. He looked at Raghubir and showed him the door.

Raghubir was extremely nervous; not knowing what to do, he sent us a telegram.

I sent him the following telegram: "Do not displease Mahatma Gandhi at any cost." And I forwarded a copy to Mahadev Desai.

Raghubir followed Gandhiji to Shantiniketan. There he took an excellent shot of Gandhiji while he was sitting next to Rabindranath Tagore. Then he went to the Ramgarh Congress and continued the shooting.

After two months he sent back the camera.

To this day I have not met Raghubir Singh.

The only reason for this person born in an affluent family to happily accept the rough and tumble of a coarse life and do the shooting for two months was Gandhiji's inimitable charisma!

~

Lionel Fielden, the first director general of All India Radio, visited Sevagram every weekend to talk to Gandhiji.

Sevagram had no connection with the outside world. Lord Irwin, the viceroy, made arrangements for telephone facilities in Sevagram, at government expense, just for the sake of communicating with Gandhiji!

~

In Sevagram, there were many small ashram buildings near Gandhiji's cottage. I found Dr. Peter Booke on the veranda of a building, reading something. Seated a little further from him was Ravishankar Shukla, the premier of the Central Provinces.

I went up to Shukla and told him that I wanted to film him and requested him to come out into the sunlight.

Shukla's response was a stern, "I do not want to be filmed."

After a few minutes, I called Dr. Booke and said, "I'll come to the veranda again. Please talk to me about my film on Gandhiji. I will respond in detail. Perhaps, Shukla may change his mind then."

Booke was our friend. He knew about our work. He did as he was told. I answered him elaborately.

Shukla, who was listening to us, asked, "Do you want to include me in the film?"

"But haven't you expressed your unwillingness?" I said.

"No, I am ready. This very minute," said Shukla

I was angry with him for not acceding to my original request readily. Being young, I possessed the mischief befitting my age.

"Please walk the length of twenty yards and turn back, only then will the sequence appear attractive," I said.

The elderly Shukla was handsome—he was six feet tall, with a light complexion and a long, grey moustache. Poor man! He walked twenty yards in the hot sun and came back. The shot, taken in bright daylight, turned out well. The Central Provinces was one among the seven states where the Congress had formed ministries.

I took silly pride in having made the premier of the Central Provinces walk up and down in the hot sun!

But what made him walk was the magic word 'Gandhi'.

5

The English and Gujarati weeklies edited by Gandhiji – *Harijan* and *Harijan Bandhu* – were published from Poona. Gopalan, a young bachelor from Tamilnadu, was the manager of these publications. I came to know him very well. Whenever I travelled from Bombay to Chennai or from Chennai to Bombay, he would meet me at the Poona railway station with fruits.

I met him in Poona before setting off to the west in search of stock shots of Gandhiji. *Harijan* had a larger number of subscribers in Europe than in America. Its circulation was barely five thousand and it carried no commercial advertisements. Gandhiji's articles were its mainstay. Gopalan got permission from his bosses and provided me the names and addresses of their foreign subscribers.

Soon after the *Harijan* was printed in Poona, the Associated Press of India and Reuters would transmit Gandhiji's articles by wire. Most of the dailies in India and abroad would carry his articles in English or their translated versions the same day. Weeklies and monthlies would publish summarised versions of the articles.

Most newspapers across the world would publish every word uttered by Gandhiji the very same day, just as they published his every written word. The speeches and writings of an individual – who had no position or wealth or authority – have never before been published consistently in this manner.

Whether it was about the freedom struggle or some constructive programme, if Gandhiji uttered a word, lakhs and lakhs of Indians acted on it with promptness and pious devotion.

He was a living example of the saying, 'The country swayed to my word.'

~

Browsing through the names of the European subscribers of the *Harijan* – that too, with the intention of writing to them and meeting them – was a new experience for me. How many lords, professors and social workers figured on the list!

I did not know any of them. But when I read through the list, I felt a sense of familiarity with regard to a few names—as though I had known them for a long time. I made a list of such persons and wrote to them. I introduced myself and informed them about my visit in connection with the film on Gandhiji. I explained my intention to seek their help and requested them to write to my Rome address.

I left Bombay by an Italian ship. On reaching Rome, I went to Thomas Cook's, where I found a number of letters waiting for me. All those to whom I had written had replied. Some had asked me to stay in their houses as their guest. Every letter overflowed with affection. They had established associations in their countries with names like 'Indian Society' or 'Gandhi Society'. In some countries, they met every week to read the *Harijan* and discuss Gandhian tenets.

In certain countries, when they came to receive me, they brought one or two press correspondents with them. Most of the European correspondents do not know English. It was possible that they might misunderstand me. Therefore, I got the information I wanted to communicate typed in English, and gave each press correspondent a copy. They gave wide publicity for the film and for me the same evening or the very next day. My work was thus made easier.

There were many friends from Europe who had stayed with me in America. There were also other friends who lived in Europe. All of them held Gandhiji in high esteem; but it could not be said that they were interested in him.

But the new friends who had written to me from Europe were all deeply involved in Gandhism and had great love for India. Some had met Gandhiji and some had even visited India. The letters of these persons gave me great joy and new strength. The circle of friends in Europe widened.

The admirers of Gandhism belonged to different countries, spoke different languages and pursued different professions. Most of them did not know one another. Yet, the spiritual power of Gandhiji united them all.

Whenever I visited a foreign country for the collection of documentary footage, I would initially stay in the most reputed hotel of that country. After completing my work I would move to a modest hotel—I found this tactic beneficial.

In Rome, I stayed in the internationally reputed Grand Hotel. The person who had checked in just before me was the famous Hollywood actor Clark Gable. The city newspapers would publish the names of persons staying in big hotels. When contacting important people, this was of great help.

There was a very big cinema studio run by the government called Cinecittà in Rome. It had five floors and they were let out to private companies. It also housed a huge laboratory.

When I went to Italy in 1939, the country was under the dictatorship of Mussolini. The government ran the news agency.

I met the chief executive of Cinecittà. Since he had seen my name in the newspapers, he received me enthusiastically and made arrangements for me to watch all the documentaries produced by them. He instructed a middle-aged man and a woman who knew English to assist me. I was the guest of Cinecittà for three days.

I spent the whole of the first day watching their excellent documentaries. The next day I asked whether they had shots of Gandhiji's visit to Italy. On the third day they screened a reel for me that I watched very eagerly. There was no sign of Gandhiji even though we were half way through the reel. Instead, the title 'Signor Grandi Arrives at New York' appeared. Grandi had been the Italian minister for foreign affairs. This film was shot when he disembarked at the New York harbour.

I remembered an incident I had heard in connection with this.

When Grandi arrived at the New York harbour, thousands had assembled to welcome him. He was astonished on seeing the crowd, but no one showed any sign of excitement on seeing him. Grandi understood the reason for the crowd from the evening newspapers. People had mistaken Grandi for Gandhi and had thronged the harbour. The papers reported that they had been very disappointed.

I said to myself sadly, "There will be nothing about Gandhiji in this reel. These people too are mistaking Grandi for Gandhi. I am unlucky." In the next frame a military band could be heard. What a surprise! Military officers received Gandhiji and escorted him very respectfully. Hundreds of children and youth of the Fascist brigade honoured Gandhiji with a march-past in military uniform. Some were marching with rifles. A few machine guns were also visible in the march-past. Gandhiji, the apostle of non-violence, saw this and smiled. That toothless smile was wonderful. Gandhiji, in simple white khadi dress, was a striking figure amidst the hundreds in military uniform.

On seeing Gandhiji, the young employees of the studio abruptly left their work and watched the film with eagerness.

This shot was 300 feet long. It included the reception given to Gandhiji by thousands of people at the Rome railway station.

I requested them to make a copy of the shots I had seen and also asked for a Mussolini clip of about thirty feet. It was a matter of courtesy.

I paid twenty pounds, that is, approximately two hundred and sixty rupees. Films could not be sent outside the country without the government's permission. The Cinecittà officials helped me get permission immediately.

I insured the film and sent it to India through Thomas Cook.

The keenness with which the young men and women working in Cinecittà watched the film sequence featuring Gandhiji is still etched in my mind.

Gandhiji was a saint who stole the hearts of people from different parts of the world!

~

The League of Nations was situated on the banks of a lovely river in Geneva, Switzerland. It was the forerunner to the United Nations Organisation. It had become defunct by the time of my visit due to the outbreak of the Second World War.

I visited the only documentary firm in Geneva. It was a small firm with a tiny office. The room was littered with odd things. Old film cans were stacked in a corner. The only person there, with a woebegone look on his face, was the proprietor.

I introduced myself and asked him whether he had any films connected with Gandhiji.

"The League of Nations was very active for many years. Leaders from across the world would visit Geneva. I used to shoot documentaries and distribute them all over the world. Now that the League is defunct, my business has suffered. I have gathered all the old films to destroy them. Drop by this afternoon and see if you can find anything useful for your purpose."

I went to his office again that afternoon. He fished out a reel from an old can. I was struck with wonder when he screened it. Only in my wildest dreams could I have imagined that I would lay my hands on such a wonderful film sequence.

When Gandhiji was a guest of Romain Rolland at the village of Villeneuve, a fine film had been shot of Gandhiji walking rapidly as usual, enjoying the scenery.

After Gandhiji initiated his struggle for India's freedom, it could be said that he lost some of his personal freedom. He could never stroll around on his own. He would always be surrounded by people. Even in this shot, Miss Slade (Mirabehn) followed him like a shadow at a distance of about thirty yards.

There was also a wonderful shot of Gandhiji delivering a lecture in Geneva with Edmund Prevert acting as the chair. There was another shot, from a different angle, of Gandhiji receiving the guard of honour given by the youth brigade in Italy.

"How much would this cost?" I asked the owner of the documentary firm.

"Pay me as much as you wish," he replied.

I gave him the usual twenty pounds.

With joy on face, he took my hands and said, "In my present position, this is a fortune. I must thank you."

"The film you had kept safe for so long is, for me, a fortune. I must thank you," I said.

If I had been delayed even by a day we would have lost this incredible treasure.

I prayed, thankful for God's boundless grace.

~

Éclair Drass was one of the famous studios of Paris. Quribe, the technical expert of the Bombay branch of Kodak, had given me an introductory letter. Quribe had earlier worked for Éclair Drass. So they treated me like a guest and made arrangements, like in Italy, for a man and a woman who knew English to help me.

With the help of Éclair Drass, I filmed Romain Rolland who was then living in Vezeley and recorded his speech.

The footage I got in Paris was also of rare value.

I came across some shots of Gandhiji arriving at, and later departing from, the Marseilles harbour, on his way to London to attend the Round Table Conference.

On his return from London to India, Gandhiji was given a grand reception in Paris. The Indian student community gave him a separate reception. A certain incident connected to this reception reveals the devotion Indian students felt for Gandhiji.

A French documentary firm approached an Indian student and offered to pay him a tidy sum if he intercepted and spoke a few words to Gandhiji when he was on his way out after addressing the students. This would give them time to film him.

Indian students living abroad were always in need of money. Yet, that student had firmly declined the offer, 'I will do nothing that might displease my nation's leader.'

I got a film clip of a popular Congress woman leader addressing a gathering of charka-spinning women when the khadi movement began in the Punjab.

I also acquired a shot in which Gandhiji appears wearing a full-length dhoti, a khadi shirt and a Gandhi cap.

I think this is the only one of its kind.

~

Romain Rolland, the Nobel laureate, was a great French intellectual and an internationally known writer. He was the first to write Gandhiji's biography—a book that made the Mahatma known abroad. I decided to record his opinions about Gandhiji and include it in our documentary.

For six months of the year, Romain Rolland lived in Villeneuve, near Geneva. He spent the rest of the year in a French village called Vezeley. He did not know English. But his wife and sister could speak English.

First, I wrote to his Villeneuve address. His sister replied that he was in Vezeley.

There was no train to Vezeley. Even tourist agents in Paris could not direct me to Vezeley. After consulting a good number of directories for about two hours, a friend in Éclair Drass told me that it was located sixteen miles from the Avalon railway station. It was about two hundred miles from Paris.

Vezeley is a tiny village situated on a hill. There is an ancient church on the top of the hill. Pilgrims visit this church everyday. Rolland's house was on the way to the church. It had a lovely garden.

An old maid answered the door and bade me sit in a room. A tiger skin was spread on the floor. A little later, Rolland's sister welcomed me and exchanged pleasantries.

She said that her brother prayed the whole morning and that I could meet him in the evening. She made arrangements for my stay in a nearby hotel.

I met Rolland in the evening. He spoke in French and his wife acted as the interpreter.

The moment I set my eyes upon him, I felt immense respect for him. He asked, "Are Gandhi, Nehru, Tagore and others fine?" I had the rare privilege of telling him that all those peerless leaders of India were in good health.

Rolland eagerly made detailed enquiries about the film. Finally he said, 'Yours is an excellent undertaking. It would be nice if you produced a film on the life of Swami Vivekananda next."

During the course of our conversation, he began to reminisce about the Indian leaders of his acquaintance.

He said, "Alas! Lajpat Rai has passed away. I have never seen an Indian as majestic as him."

Then he talked to me about Jagdish Chandra Bose and about Subash Chandra Bose who was then the Congress president.

While having tea I requested him to speak on Gandhiji for our film. He said, "I will speak, you can record it. But, please, do not film me. I'll appear ugly on screen."

"The people of India have heard a lot about you. Your book on Gandhiji has been translated into many Indian languages. Indians will be overjoyed to see you in the film," I said. Then I pleaded with his wife to get him to agree. She won him over, at last. I booked a trunk call to Paris immediately. Charles Martin, the cinematographer, arrived with a camera and a recording truck the very next day.

Romain Rolland spoke twice. Then I took leave of him and left for Paris.

I sent the film to a laboratory in Paris for developing. War broke out before it could be developed and all the studios and laboratories were closed. After a great deal of effort we recovered most of the film we shot of Rolland and included it in the documentary. A small part of it is still in France, not yet developed. We could include in the documentary only that portion which we were able to retrieve.

We got library shots of the coronation of King George V held in 1911 in Delhi from the Norman Film Library in London. It is a historical record of our nation having been under British rule. The cost of ordinary film clips was two shillings per foot. This one, preserved for its rarity, cost me five shillings.

I went to the news agency called the British Paramount News in London and enquired about documentaries relating to India. They asked me to come the next day. When I went the next day, they asked me to come the day after. Finally, they said that I would have to pay one pound per foot for the available stock that was 180 feet long. The price quoted was exorbitant. I said that I was prepared to pay the quoted price, but would buy only the portion I required.

They had not expected me to agree to their price. After thinking over it for some time, they said, "This is a political film. You may use it against the British in India and other countries. So whatever amount you may pay, we don't want to sell it."

Such a response, from a firm doing business with profit as its raison d'etre, is a glowing example of British patriotism. Though I was sorely disappointed, I was also amazed by their patriotism.

At the same time, I was deeply pained at the thought of those Indians who indulged in propaganda against our mother country, when Gandhiji and lakhs and lakhs of men and women were suffering in horrifying prisons for attempting to break the chains of foreign rule.

In this connection I am reminded of an incident narrated by my New York friend Gordon P. Halstead.

Halstead and his wife had worked as teachers in a school run by an American in Allahabad. Since they were close friends of the Nehru family and showed interest in the freedom movement, the British government deported them.

After going to America, the Halsteads evinced more interest in the Indian independence movement.

When I left New York by ship in 1937, Halstead could not come and see me off. Instead, he sent me a packet. The words *'Inquilab Zindabad'* were written on it. It was then one of the nationalist slogans of India. Inside the packet I found a khadi tricolour flag!

The following incident was narrated by Halstead:

> During the war, when Gandhiji and lakhs of Indians were in jail, the British government sent Sir A. Ramaswamy Mudaliar, who possessed extra-ordinary oratorical skills for propaganda on their behalf.
>
> Four or five of us, all friends of India, vowed to defeat the propaganda of Ramaswamy Mudaliar.
>
> We were continuously getting information about the situation in India from our Indian friends and Americans living in India. We were fairly well aware of the real condition of the nation.

Ramaswamy Mudaliar's first speech was scheduled to take place in New York. We were there well in advance and we managed to seat ourselves in different places in the hall. American tradition requires that at the end of the lecture the orator must field the questions put forth by the audience. The orator should not indulge in prevarication. After the oration we shot a volley of questions from all directions. The propagandist had least expected such questions and he struggled to answer them. Even the one or two answers he gave did not satisfy the audience.

We did not stop with this. We went wherever he gave lectures and made him fumble miserably for words.

The lectures did not produce the intended result. Actually, it was in direct contrast to what the British had expected. Mudaliar left America soon.

Halstead became emotionally excited.

No doubt, even Americans were awestruck at the oratorical skills of Ramaswamy Mudaliar. But however powerful the rhetoric may be, if used improperly and for selfish ends it will never bring victory.

'Truth is God,' is Gandhiji's maxim.

6

"Gandhi is the greatest man in the whole world," said an American friend.

I did not respond.

"Do you know why I say that?"

"No," I said.

He explained:

When Gandhiji went to London to attend the Round Table Conference, two famous Americans went there to invite him to America.

The management of an internationally famous hotel offered to set apart an entire floor for Gandhiji and his entourage, free of cost. It was also ready to undertake the onerous task of providing him with food, including goat's milk. Further, as was the custom when foreign dignitaries stayed, the hotel agreed to hoist India's national flag during the period of Gandhiji's stay.

An American broadcasting company offered to donate a day's income if Gandhiji agreed to speak for five minutes on radio. (There were many private broadcasting companies in America. They charged huge amounts for using radio time.)

A popular American daily came forward to donate a hundred thousand dollars to the Gandhi Fund, if Gandhiji permitted one of their correspondents to be with him during his stay.

But Mahatma Gandhi declined the invitation saying that he had no time. On their request, he sent a message to the people of America.

Until then, never had a leader declined an invitation to visit America. Some craved for a chance to visit America. Some solicited invitations. Gandhiji was the only leader who did not visit America despite the country inviting him sincerely.

"That's why I called him the world's greatest person," concluded my American friend.

~

John Haynes Holmes, a famous Christian priest, was one of the two men who went to London to invite Gandhiji to America.

He was a priest at the community church situated at the heart of New York. Every Sunday he wore a Gandhi cap and delivered his sermon to a congregation of thousands in the large auditorium of the church. I had an opportunity to listen to his sermon when I was a student.

He was the foremost among the distinguished persons who vigorously propagated Gandhism in America all their lives. He had visited India many times and had had discussions with Gandhiji. He also wrote a book comparing Gandhiji with Jesus Christ.

When I went to New York in 1939, I wrote to him expressing my desire to record his speech on film for the Gandhi documentary. His secretary replied that Holmes was in a hospital and he regretted his inability to accede to my request.

In 1953, when the Gandhi film was screened for the press in New York, Holmes was among those who saw it from beginning to end, and was moved to tears.

Pathe News was one of the five documentary news companies in America. In 1937, as a student, I had the rare opportunity of undergoing training in this internationally reputed company.

Twice a week, work would begin at nine in the night. Documentaries received from various parts of the world would be screened. There would be no time to develop and take prints of films that arrived late. So the negatives would be screened—white would appear black, and black, white.

Commentary writers would work as they watched the film. Commentators would read the voice-over.

The documentary would then be screened again. The sound room was located opposite to the screen. Sophisticated equipment worth lakhs of dollars were in that sound-proof glass-panelled room. An expert was in charge of the equipment.

While the film was being screened, the technician had to arrange several sound tracks carrying recordings of speech, commentary, music and sound effects, in synchronisation with the visuals. This task is akin to performing ashtavadanam.* When the commentary is being read, the music must be tuned down. The volume of music must be increased gradually as the commentary comes to an end. The technician must handle – with meticulous care – innumerable sound effects, like that of an aeroplane taking off, or a train running on the tracks, or people clapping jubilantly.

For every documentary they would take two sound negatives. If one were to get damaged the second could be used. The expert in the sound room was very kind to me. He allowed me the responsibility of taking the second sound negative. He would supervise my work carefully and rectify my mistakes immediately.

This special training benefited me in many ways. Specifically, I gained first-hand experience in documentary production.

During my visit to America the next year, I went to Pathe News to collect stock shots. My old friends received me warmly. The manager of the news section said, "We will keep the library open for you. Take all that you need." He instructed his people to collect all shots connected with Gandhiji and India.

I went there the next day. They had collected 1080 feet of film! Whatever I could not get in London was available here. There were many shots that I had not expected or even dreamt of finding.

In the American soil never visited by Gandhiji, there was so much film on him! One clipping was of his speech in a town called Borsad during the Dandi Salt March. It had been filmed and recorded by an American. Sound was still new to India then. Gandhiji's talk on khadi was not clear, but with some effort it could be followed.

That clipping, shot in 1930, was Gandhiji's first recorded speech on film.

---

* Ashtavadanam is an art form where the artist performs eight different feats – such as reciting and composing verse, playing chess, answering questions, etc. – simultaneously before an audience.

Another invaluable shot I got from Pathe News was the speech of Vithalbhai Patel. He was also a barrister and freedom fighter like his younger brother Sardar Vallabhbhai Patel. He had been in jail several times and had served as chair of the imperial legislative council during the British period. An intrepid man, he had once ordered the police out of the council premises.

When he went to America, the city fathers of New York gave him a reception. Pathe News had shot and recorded his speech with superb clarity. He spoke in his usual emphatic and unambiguous manner:

> It is said that Mahatma Gandhi is opposed to the political representation of the Untouchables. Nothing is farther from the truth. He objects only to the method by which the representation is sought to be made.

~

I asked the company executive how much I had to pay. With a smile, he said that 80 of the 1080 feet was the company's compliment.

I expressed my gratitude.

He continued, "Can we fix a dollar per foot for the rest?"

I was silent. A dollar was worth three rupees in those days.

"All right. Pay five hundred dollars. That would do."

I thanked him again. I paid the money at once, and insured and sent the film to India through Thomas Cook.

Since I had undergone training in Pathe News, I could get these rare shots easily and without much delay, at a good price. I had the satisfaction that my visit to America had not been wasted. We made use of this entire lot of film in the documentary.

~

The New York Public Library is one of the world's largest libraries. There is no place more suited to appease one's hunger for knowledge. In this library that houses lakhs of books, there were about two hundred books on Gandhiji in English and other European languages! (There are more than two thousand now.)

I met the director of the library and expressed my wish to film all the books on Gandhiji. He directed Freehaver, one of his assistants, to help me. Freehaver collected all the books and I tried to figure out a way of capturing them on film.

The New York Institute of Photography where I had studied was close by. It is one of the world's largest schools of photography and cinematography. I met one of my teachers there and asked for his advice. He was an American of German origin. With a smile, he said, "Don't worry. I will come and help you," and started for the library with a good movie camera and arc-lamps.

First we shot the books together, then we shot them in different lots, and lastly we shot the jackets and inside pages of a number of books.

Some of the visitors to the library watched the shooting curiously. There was one Indian student among them. An American lady even asked me, "Are you Mr. Gandhi?"

The job was over. I thanked my teacher. I rejoiced at my luck in having a teacher like him.

I then collected the catalogue cards of the books and filmed them.

Even in those days there were more than two hundred books in that library on a man who had never set foot on the American soil!

~

A few years later, my friend Perumal Mudaliar, the principal of the Teachers' College at Saidapet, Chennai, invited me to a function held there. The chief guest was an Indian and his wife was an American. I was introduced to both of them.

The chief guest said to me, "I know you. I saw you and conversed with you when you were filming the books on Mahatma Gandhi at the New York Public Library. I was a student then. But you may not remember me."

This person was Dr. S. Chandrasekhar who later became a minister of the Government of India and the vice chancellor of Annamalai University.

~

I was educated and formally trained in photography and cinematography. Yet, I lacked experience and therefore the confidence to undertake a great work like producing a documentary on Gandhiji.

I was not particular about doing the work myself, but was firm that the film should be excellent. So I employed the best cinematographers in India, France, America and other countries.

I planned to shoot for the film in South Africa. Good cameramen were hard to find there. Our finances did not permit my taking a cinematographer from India. Further, in South Africa, we only needed to shoot the important places connected with Gandhiji. So I decided to go alone.

For shooting in South Africa I planned to buy a handy DeVry movie camera made in America. It could hold a 100-foot roll and shoot 20 feet at one cranking.

I went to the DeVry firm in New York. There were two cameras on display.

I showed my visiting card to the young man there. He received me cordially and showed me the cameras. He quoted the price and then asked me whether I could come the next day.

The next day he gave me a forty per cent discount on the bill. I had not expected this, I was stunned.

Observing my surprise, he said, "I am authorised to give only a twenty-five per cent discount. I wished to help you, so I contacted our head office in Chicago yesterday and got permission to give you a larger discount."

I thanked him and asked, "May I know what prompted you to help me?"

"I lived in Chennai for two years. On seeing your card, I was gripped by old memories. I like the people of Chennai," he said.

He meant the people of Chennai of forty years ago!

~

Most people desire to visit foreign countries. And there are people who think that going to America is going to heaven. Only later will they see the hell in that heaven.

While studying in America, I benefited from the experience in many ways. I am grateful for that. But at the same time, I cannot forget the miseries I underwent because of racism.

Now, there was a compelling need to go to South Africa, the birthplace of apartheid. Bound by duty, I made the trip.

Two things are abundant in South Africa: delicious fruits and horrifying apartheid.

Gandhiji was a victim of the cruelties of apartheid. He had been much wounded by the cane lashes and cruel kicks of the whites.

Once, when Gandhiji reached South Africa by ship, a frenzied white mob tried to kill him. The man who rescued him from that great danger was also a white.

General Smuts was then the prime minister of South Africa. His brother's son, Adrian Smuts, was among the six hundred students residing in a hostel called New York International House. I was also a resident of the hostel and I met him there often. When I toured America with some of my friends, he was also there with his friends and we met a few times. He said that he was not racist and requested me to be his guest whenever I happened to visit South Africa.

Adrian Smuts was a schoolteacher in Cape Town. I was going to South Africa two years after our last meeting. I wrote to him and also sent a telegram from the ship. I expected to see him or at least to receive a message—but was sorely disappointed.

Apartheid was so rampant that he could not even receive his coloured friend!

I stayed as the guest of A.D. Lazarus, a Tamil Christian from Durban. I had met him when he was in America for higher studies. He was working as a teacher in Shastri College in Durban. Later, he became the principal of the college.

The senior Lazarus was Gandhiji's friend. He had actively participated in the struggles organised by Gandhiji and had also been imprisoned. In the early days he had lived in a small village near the Natal border. During the struggle, the satyagrahis had camped in his house.

From Durban, the senior Lazarus and I drove in a motorcar—along the route taken by Gandhiji with the satyagrahis. On the way he stopped the car at a particular place and narrated a heart-rending incident:

> Under the leadership of Gandhiji, hundreds of us were marching across the Natal border to defy the law by entering the Transvaal without permits. Many were women. Mostly Tamils. All were illiterate casual labourers. An infant died on the march. The mother immediately dug a pit, buried the baby and followed us without looking back. When Gandhiji went to console her, she said, "We have not come to fight for the dead. We are fighting for the living. Let us march ahead without looking back."

Manilal, one of Gandhiji's sons, and his wife, Sushilabehn, were living in the Phoenix Settlement where Gandhiji had once lived. I filmed the Settlement. Gandhiji did penance for some time in the central prison of Pretoria. I filmed the prison too.

Kruger, the president of South Africa, had lived in Johannesburg. Gandhiji used to go for walks on the street where Kruger lived. One day a watchman new to the president's palace pushed Gandhiji down and kicked him.

Coates, who knew Gandhiji, was riding a horse up that street. He said, "Mr. Gandhi, I saw what happened with my own eyes. Proceed against him in court, I will stand witness."

Gandhiji replied, "I am firm that I will not go to court with regard to any personal grievance."

I had read about all these incidents in Gandhiji's autobiography. Fortunately, the condition is not so bad now. I filmed the place where Gandhiji had been beaten.

Recently, I read a note Gandhiji had written about Kruger: "Even illiterates have ruled big empires. Kruger, who was the president of South Africa, did not even know how to sign his name."

General Smuts, the prime minister of South Africa, was no general. During the Boer War he was the sworn enemy of the British. In order to win him over, the British conferred several honorary titles on him. When the British were engaged in a war with Egypt he participated in it. The British had then conferred the title 'General' on him.

General Botha was the president of South Africa at that time. On getting to know about the title, he had sent a telegram to Smuts in Egypt: "You and I know you are no general."

General Smuts, the iron man of South Africa, who had put Gandhiji in jail several times, not only became Gandhiji's friend towards the end, but also praised him as 'the greatest man of South Africa'.

~

Hermann Kallenbach, a close friend of Gandhiji, was a German architect settled in South Africa. He played a significant part in Gandhiji's experiments and struggles.

Once, Gandhiji and Kallenbach went to England from South Africa by ship. Kallenbach had a pair of binoculars that cost seven pounds. Every day Gandhiji argued that those who observed austerity should not possess such expensive articles, "Why don't we throw away these binoculars which cause quarrels between us?"

Kallenbach replied, "Yes, we could do that." So Gandhiji threw the binoculars into the sea.

Gandhiji wrote in his autobiography that Kallenbach had a plan to settle in India. But the plan did not materialise. "Could he have come to India, he would have been leading today the simple happy life of a farmer and weaver. Now he is in South Africa, leading his old life and doing brisk business as an architect."

I met Kallenbach when he was still busily engaged in his profession. I stayed with him for a day. In South Africa, his was the only white man's house in which I stayed.

Kallenbach took me in his car to Tolstoy Farm which was a few miles from Johannesburg. Gandhiji started his ashram life in that place, bought by Kallenbach. After Gandhiji returned to India, Kallenbach sold it to a white South African.

Kallenbach introduced me to the families living on that farm. Nobody shook hands with me. They gave us tea. The lady of the house handed Kallenbach's cup to him and left mine beside me.

While coming out, Kallenbach apologised to me. I pointed out to him, "They allowed me to enter the farm only because of you. I am indebted to you for that."

The farm was vast. I shot for half an hour. Kallenbach carried the camera tripod all along. He would not listen to my objections. I was moved by this great man's devotion and reverence for Gandhiji.

7

From South Africa, the birthplace of apartheid, I sailed to Bombay. It was very difficult for Indians to get accommodation in first class. I could get a berth only after a big struggle. There were two berths in my cabin. From Durban to Mombasa, Kenya, I travelled alone.

From Mombasa an Indian Muslim barrister travelled with me. He was serving as the chief presidency magistrate in Bombay. He had come to Kenya to meet his relations.

He was a man of fine qualities. He was about fifty, older than me by twenty years. He had married a Parsi woman under the condition that their daughter would be married to a Parsi. On reaching Bombay, he introduced his wife and son to me. I learnt a lot during the ten days I travelled with him. It was my good fortune that I could travel with him.

One day, when we were talking about Gandhiji, he said in English, "Gandhi made a force without a force."

~

As soon as the ship reached Bombay, an immigration officer checked my passport and stamped 'Permitted to land'. Permission for me to enter my own mother country!

I went to the National Hindu Hotel where I usually stayed. A telegram was awaiting me—I read the message eagerly. The two-word telegram made me extremely happy.

The telegram was from Kovai Ayyamuthu who was then staying in Chettinadu as a guest in the house of one of the directors of our company. He had sent the telegram on getting to know about my arrival: "Welcome Home – Ayyamuthu and Friends."

In those days telegrams were sent only to announce calamity or death. Telegrams welcoming people were quite rare.

Imagine my happiness on receiving such a telegram when I reached my homeland after wandering all over the world for about six months.

This telegram was not for me; it was for the saintly duty I had undertaken.

~

Our film on Gandhiji was based on the newsreel tradition. Until we made our film, no documentary had been produced in India. How, then, was our documentary produced?

The years between 1917 and 1947 were the golden period of the Indian independence movement. It could also be called the Gandhian era. Gandhiji returned to India triumphantly after proving the efficacy of satyagraha in South Africa. Bharati, the great poet, had described the condition of our countrymen thus: "They die of fear, again and again. There is nothing in this world they are not afraid of."

Gandhiji turned these cowardly people into human beings—warriors. In thirty years, with these men whom he made out of dust, employing non-violence as the only weapon, Gandhiji wrested the country's freedom from Britain—the most powerful nation in the history of the world.

In the years 1921, 1930 and 1940, there were momentous struggles under the leadership of Gandhiji. The annual Congress meetings held every year in various parts of the country infused new vigour in the people.

Attracted by Gandhiji's simplicity, sincerity, spirituality and charismatic smile, lakhs and lakhs of people followed him, as if mesmerised. No sacrifice was too big for them.

Patriotic fervour knew no bounds. Fear diminished among the people. Film producers were motivated to film the deliberations of the Congress conferences and they showed them to the people in every nook and corner of the country. They filmed the conferences held in Kakinada (1923), Gaya (1925), Chennai (1927), Calcutta (1938), Lahore (1929), Karachi (1930), Bombay (1934), Haripura (1938), Tripuri (1939) and Ramgarh (1940). Gandhiji was the centre of attraction in all these conferences.

All the nationalist documentaries produced in those days revolved around Gandhiji.

The Dandi March, Gandhiji's departure for the Round Table Conference, his return to Bombay from London, his Harijan Yatra, his Frontier Yatra and a few meetings of the All India Congress Committee too were filmed.

Foreign cinematographers had shot the grand receptions given to Gandhiji in England and Europe during his trip to attend the Round Table Conference.

I think that our documentary was the first in the world on an individual who had neither power nor wealth.

~

Venkaiah of Andhra had filmed the 1923 Kakinada Congress. Dr. Pathy and his brother found out, after much effort, that he had died a few years earlier due to some mental illness. We could not trace his family nor could we find who had commissioned the film and what had happened to it.

The readers will remember how the studio owner in Lahore had cheated us by sending a few film bits purported to be library shots of the Gaya Congress.

Quite fortunately, we could get shots of the 1927 Chennai Congress. C.N. Muthuranga Mudaliar was the chairman of the reception committee and Dr. Ansari was the president of the Chennai Congress. S. Srinivasa Iyengar of Mylapore, who had presided over the Guwahati Congress, was the life and soul of this conference. Gandhiji and Maulana Mohammed Ali appear in this film. Pandit Jawaharlal Nehru also appears for the first time in a film. He looks young and rather attractive.

Aurora Film Corporation of Calcutta had produced this film. Ramaseshan was the manager of their Chennai branch. The cinematographer of the film was Jiten Bannerjee, a Bengali settled in Chennai.

When we screened the Gandhi film in Chennai, Jiten Bannerjee was overwhelmed with joy and thanked us for including his work in the film.

The historic Vedaranyam Salt Satyagraha took place in 1930. Volunteers walked from Trichy to Vedaranyam under the leadership of Rajaji. It ranks next only to the Dandi Satyagraha.

It is our misfortune that there was no producer in Tamilnadu who was patriotic and bold enough to film this holy satyagraha.

The Calcutta Congress took place in 1928. A huge procession was organised to welcome Motilal Nehru, who presided over it. Subash Chandra Bose, the icon of the youth, was the commander-in-chief of the volunteers. He appears very majestic in military uniform.

Of course, the centre of attraction was Gandhiji. Bose receiving Kasturba respectfully at the Calcutta railway station is a feast for the eyes.

An all party conference was also held to coincide with the Calcutta Congress. Annie Besant, Sapru, Jayakar, Dr. Radhakrishnan, T.R. Venkatrama Shastri, G.A. Natesan, Sir C.P. Ramaswamy Iyer and others appear in the film.

The All India Congress Committee meeting held in Calcutta in 1939 had also been filmed.

Jawaharlal Nehru's speech had been filmed. Nehru spoke in a subdued manner. His first sentence was: "India has many problems today, but the outstanding problem is how to pull together."

At the same time Subash Chandra Bose was filmed in a studio and his impressive speech was also recorded in connection with the inauguration of the Forward Bloc within the Congress.

When our film was screened in Tamilnadu, a touring theatre was booked in Chidambaram for five days. Unexpectedly, the film ran for seven days. The students of Annamalai University saw it two or three times to memorise the speech of Subash Babu.

The speech that cast a spell ran thus:

> Forward Bloc has come into existence because the country needs it and the time is ripe for it. Our struggle is no doubt a non-violent struggle. But even a non-violent struggle needs an army, an organisation and machinery.

~

The Lahore Congress was held in 1929. Pandit Jawaharlal Nehru presided over it. Motilal Nehru, the outgoing president, passed the responsibility to his son.

Gandhiji was the focus of interest. Several important leaders like S. Srinivasa Iyengar and Subash Chandra Bose attended it. The resolution of 'Purna Swaraj' as the goal of the Congress was passed.

The same people who had filmed this Congress produced another excellent film in 1939, of Gandhiji's journey to the North West Frontier.

Gandhiji converted the belligerent Pathans into non-violent soldiers. Khan Abdul Ghaffar Khan, the leader of the Pathans, was a majestic person, towering over six feet. In this film we can see him leading Gandhiji by the hand, as if he were a child. Ghaffar Khan took his special guest and his followers around in an exclusively arranged bus. In one scene Gandhiji can be seen crossing a river.

The wonderful scene of thousands of Pathans welcoming Gandhiji amidst the beautiful surroundings of the Frontier is unforgettable.

In 1930, the Congress met in Karachi. I believe the Karachi Congress was the only one held outside, in the open.

The president of the Congress was Sardar Vallabhbhai Patel. Gandhiji occupied the central place on the dais.

In the film, there is a scene showing the Bengali leader Sen Gupta and his foreign wife Nellie arriving at the Karachi railway station.

At Karachi, the Congress unanimously elected Gandhiji as its sole representative at the Second Round Table Conference.

Bombay is the capital of the Indian film world. Bombay stood first in the production of nationalist films. Dadasaheb Phalke, the father of Indian cinema, was also born there.

Gandhiji had talks with Viceroy Irwin in New Delhi. The Gandhi–Irwin Pact was signed. Arrangements were made for Gandhiji to leave for London from Bombay. But due to a hitch that arose in concluding the pact, Gandhiji missed the Bombay train and it was feared that he would not be able to board the *Rajputana* leaving for London. There was no air service in those days.

Sir Prabhushankar Pattani, a devotee of Gandhiji and the diwan of a native province of Saurashtra, arranged a special train, with only one third class compartment, exclusively for Gandhiji.

~

A grand reception awaited Gandhiji at the Bombay railway station. It was raining incessantly. They filmed Gandhiji addressing the people in the pouring rain. Only the face of Gandhiji and those of a few others standing near him can be seen in the film. Of the thousands who were listening to him, not a single face was visible. Everybody was holding an umbrella. The sea of humans looked like a sea of umbrellas. The torrential love showered on Gandhiji by thousands of people was more copious than the rains granted by the god Varuna!

~

The Second Round Table Conference was not a success. Gandhiji said, "I return empty-handed. But I did not compromise on the interests of the country." The mammoth reception that the people of Bombay gave Gandhiji, who returned empty-handed, was unparalleled!

Even before Gandhiji's ship reached the Bombay harbour, the British government had unleashed a reign of terror. Jawaharlal Nehru, T.A.K. Sherwani and others had been arrested. At the Bombay harbour, woe-struck Mother Kasturba and Kamala Nehru were waiting for Gandhiji. Following the footsteps of their husbands, these exemplary women too had suffered imprisonment. The picture of these two women waiting, they who were role models to the Indian womenfolk, is heart-rending! They evoke an unconscious reverence in us.

The moment Gandhiji disembarked from the ship, Kamala Nehru rushed towards him like a daughter and, keeping pace with his fast steps, poured out her heart. Everybody found this scene moving.

There was a procession of thousands of men and women volunteers. All along the way they had put up numerous welcome arches. Innumerable admirers garlanded him. They showered flowers on him as he entered Mani Bhavan. There is a scene showing Rajaji in a private conversation with Gandhiji. This was the first time that Rajaji appeared in a nationalist film.

Soon Gandhiji was arrested. Repression reigned unchecked all over the country.

Due to continued repression, after the Karachi Congress in 1930, the Bombay Congress was held only in 1934.

Bombay gave an exceptionally grand welcome to the Congress president, Rajendra Prasad, the noble son of Bihar. The repression of three years had only increased the people's enthusiasm.

The famous Ranjit Studio of Bombay shot the Bombay Congress using about six thousand feet of film. They also recorded the speeches of Gandhiji and other leaders. Gandhiji had stated: "One cannot reproduce the same thing twice. But if he does, it becomes a feat of memory and not coming out of his soul."

Till then nobody had made such a lengthy film on any Congress conference. The credit goes to Chandulal Shah, a partner in the Ranjit Film Studio.

I approached Chandulal Shah for a few scenes from this film. He said, very strictly, that I should pay four rupees per foot irrespective of whether the film was mute or had sound recording.

I paid Rs 800 for the two hundred feet of film I required.

It was a Gujarati who charged the highest price for footage on Gandhi.

~

Subash Chandra Bose was the president of the 1938 Haripura Congress. Sardar Vallabhbhai Patel was the chairman of the reception committee. This was the first conference to be held in a village according to the wishes of Gandhiji.

The president of the Congress was taken in a chariot drawn by more than fifty oxen. Gandhiji and Nehru participated in the procession.

I had the rare opportunity of photographing the proceedings of this conference.

The Chicago Radio and Telephone Company of Bombay filmed this conference. The founder of this company was Motwani, from the Sind Province. His son Nanak Motwani was a patriotic young man.

The person who filmed the Haripura Congress was Dr. Pathy. I did not know him then. With Pathy's help we got the required shots of the Haripura Congress at a reasonable rate.

In Bombay, for about twenty years, Nanak Motwani had provided public address systems free of cost to large Congress meetings. He would personally supervise the arrangements. But there was a despicable fault in him. He utilised these opportunities to gain publicity for his company. He would hang a big board with the title of his company 'Chicago' over the mike. When photographed or filmed, this board would obstruct the face of everybody, including that of Gandhiji.

Once, Nehru got angry on seeing the board. He said, 'Nanak, take this board away, at once.' Nanak trembled in fear and removed the board immediately. But the very next day he hung the board a little lower. This vulgar craze for publicity was like a disease! But for this unpardonable flaw, his patriotism was commendable.

The most famous 1942 Congress was held in Bombay. The slogan 'Quit India' coined by Gandhiji gained historic importance.

Nanak Motwani filmed this historic conference uninterruptedly. Spending thousands of rupees, he shot a documentary of about eight thousand feet. When the police arrested Gandhiji all of a sudden, they seized the film rolls as well. The wretches did not stop with that, they burnt them entirely.

The documentary was a testimony to Motwani's devotion to Gandhiji and the nation.

~

Tripuri was the second village where a Congress was held. Subash Chandra Bose was the president. The senior leaders did not approve of his style of functioning. They, who were refusing to cooperate with the British, began their non-cooperation with Subash Chandra Bose. They refused to go to the dais and remained seated among the delegates.

Gandhiji did not attend this conference. He was on a fast in Rajkot. When Nehru announced that Gandhiji had given up the fast, people welcomed the news with thunderous applause.

Several thousands of people and more than fifty caparisoned elephants participated in the procession.

It was in this conference that Rajaji described Subash Chandra Bose's speech as a 'leaking boat'!

We could get film clippings of this conference too at a reasonable price.

Maulana Abul Kalam Azad presided over the 1940 Ramgarh Congress. Our cameraman Raghubir Singh filmed it for us. Several others also filmed this conference.

Shots of this conference, other film clippings taken with Gandhiji as the main focus, library shots I had collected abroad and the ten thousand feet of film we shot ourselves constituted the documentary we made.

Sometimes we bought films in bulk. We then made negatives of the required portions. We bought about twenty thousand feet of film in such a manner.

We made arrangements for screening all these films in a theatre in Dadar, Bombay. The fee for screening a thousand feet was one rupee. Five thousand feet of film could be viewed in a day. But we could do that only after the third show of the cinema, at about half past midnight.

These shots had been made with box cameras. If people moved from the right to left, they were shot from left to right; that too, at high speed. If one watched this continuously, a headache was guaranteed.

We experienced such headaches continuously for four days. But some scenes had been shot so beautifully that we feasted our eyes on them.

The chance to see films on Gandhiji, running up to thousands of feet, was a boon.

~

At long last the task of collecting films came to an end. But unexpectedly we faced a financial crunch.

From the beginning it had been the practice of film distributors to advance money to the producers and get it back after the release of the film.

In Chennai, S.S. Vasan, the proprietor of *Ananda Vikatan,* was producing films under the banner Gemini Pictures, and was also financing films. We decided to approach him.

I met Vasan in Chennai. He received me warmly. I described the purpose of my visit. He said, "Show me a reel after producing it the way you would like to produce the entire film. If it is to my liking, we will jointly produce the film." He then added in English, "We will put our heads together."

I told him that ours was a completely different kind of film and that the efforts required for making one reel would be the same as needed for the whole film. Vasan did not accept my argument. I had gone for finance, not advice.

I informed one of the directors of our company about the situation over the phone. He said, "We have suffered a lot. Let us suffer a little more."

I forgot about my visit to Vasan; but he did not. Later, I came to know that he had harboured the incident in his mind with some rancour.

When the film was screened in Tamilnadu, all the papers published reviews immediately. But *Ananda Vikatan*'s review came after a month's time.

Kalki Krishnamurthy explained to me later, "There were several reasons for my leaving *Ananda Vikatan*. One reason was the review of the Gandhi film. I wrote my review the day it was released. But Vasan deliberately delayed publishing the review for a month. That's why I wrote in the review that nobody was going to see the film after reading the review."

Had we accepted financial help from Vasan, he would have insisted on producing the film according to his wishes. We could not have functioned independently, following our plans.

God saved us with his benign interference.

~

In Bombay, Rao Bahadur S.V. Chari and I were staying in the same hotel. He was from Tirunelveli and was about sixty years old. He had served for many years on the editorial board of the *Statesman*. By virtue of his profession, he knew a lot of people, including Gandhiji. He wrote very good English and had travelled to many countries. He showed interest in our Gandhi film and was affectionate towards me. I learnt a lot from him.

He had resigned from the *Statesman* and was working for a not-so-famous English newspaper published from Bombay. The remuneration was poor and his financial position was not quite happy.

His love for his native place – that is, his attachment to Tirunelveli – was excessive! He would walk to a hotel run by a Tirunelveli man, however far off it might be. Though he had lived in Calcutta for many years, his affinity for his place of birth – our Tirunelveli – had not diminished even a little bit.

He once said, "Chettiar, I am thinking of giving up my Rao Bahadur title. This title is an encumbrance. If I approach anybody for a loan of ten rupees they ask me, 'Sir, you are a Rao Bahadur, are you mocking us?' "

He asked me for a loan of ten rupees. When I said that I would definitely not lend any money to him, he turned gloomy.

I said, "I refused to give you a loan. But I didn't say I would not give you money. I'll pay you fifty rupees now if you write for me the events in Gandhiji's life in chronological order."

He was incredibly pleased! He finished the work the very next day.

While editing the film, whenever we had doubts, his account of Gandhiji's life was of immense help.

When the film was released, he wrote a beautiful article in English. He narrated an interesting incident from Gandhiji's life.

When Gandhiji undertook his 21-day fast in Poona, Chari went there as the correspondent of the *Statesman*. The editor had doubts about Gandhiji surviving the fast. He had composed a four-page article on Gandhiji's life and kept it ready. He had made preparations to publish it as a supplement the moment Gandhiji ceased breathing.

But the editor of the *Statesman* was to be disappointed.

The poor man did not know that the freedom of India was Gandhiji's last breath.

8

For a few years, Gandhiji lived in the Sabarmati Ashram situated on the banks of the river Sabarmati near Ahmedabad. The city of Ahmedabad became the headquarters of Gandhian activities, attracting attention from all over the world.

Kanu Desai, the famous artist, lived in Ahmedabad. He and his wife had studied at Rabindranath Tagore's Shantiniketan. The hospitable Desais lived in a beautiful house and led a simple life. I had the opportunity of associating with this patriotic couple.

Kanu Desai had served as the art director of the Gujarati film *Ram Rajya* produced in Bombay. On his request, Gandhiji saw a part of that film. It became the only Hindi film seen and enjoyed by Gandhiji. He also saw a portion of the American film *Woodrow Wilson* in Bombay.

Kanu Desai gave me an excellent photograph of Gandhiji riding a bicycle over the Sabarmati Bridge. It was he who had taken that snapshot. Kaka Kalelkar has narrated an interesting incident related to this photograph in his book *Glimpse of Gandhiji.*

Gandhiji was then living in the Sabarmati Ashram. The executive meeting of a national institution, of which Gandhiji was the president, had been arranged in a building situated on the other side of the river.

Since the car promised by Kalelkar did not arrive at the appointed time Gandhiji began to walk. It was very hot. Somebody came riding a bicycle from the opposite direction. Though he was a stranger, Gandhiji requested him to lend his bicycle. The man was dumbfounded and he handed over the bicycle with reverential awe.

Gandhiji had learnt cycling in South Africa several years ago. The stranger, however, feared that Gandhiji might fall down and therefore ran after him protectively.

Kalelkar has beautifully described the odd sight of a bare-bodied Gandhiji arriving punctually for the meeting on a bicycle.

Gandhiji valued punctuality highly and observed it very strictly.

This bicycle ride is an example of his punctuality.

~

In 1938, I travelled from Chennai to Rangoon by ship. The ship's doctor was a young man from Tamilnadu and we soon became friends. I mentioned that I was planning to shoot Gandhiji's birthplace, Porbandar, for my film. At once, he said, "My uncle, Captain Raja Iyer, is in Porbandar. He is very influential there. I will give you a letter of introduction." The young man was none other than the now famous doctor, V.S. Subramaniam.

A visit to Porbandar became necessary in 1939. I wished to shoot the general appearance of the town and then the particular street on which Gandhiji's house stood, followed by the house where he was born and its present condition. I did not want to just show a photograph of the house.

I sent Dr. Pathy alone to Porbandar, as it would have cost more for both of us to make the trip. I gave him the letter written by Dr. V.S. Subramaniam to Captain Raja Iyer and another introduction letter that I had written.

Porbandar was a native state, located close to the sea. As it was wartime, there was a strict government order that prohibited photographing or filming seaside settlements.

Pathy was unable to do his work. On his return, he said, "I couldn't shoot for the film. But I tasted the delicious Tamil food prepared by Captain Raja Iyer's wife."

Finally, we could show only a photograph of Gandhiji's house that had been published in a Gujarati paper.

~

Vande Mataram was one of the leading Gujarati nationalist dailies published from Bombay. Gandhiji's nephew, Shamaldas Gandhi, was its editor. I met him at his house in Khar, a remote part of Bombay. I borrowed a large colour portrait of Kaba Gandhi, Gandhiji's father, and brought it to Bombay by car. After shooting it on film, I returned the portrait.

~

We decided to begin our film with a historical perspective. First, we showed the graceful face of the magnificent but mutilated statue of the Buddha found in Taxila. Then we showed the Asoka pillar, the palaces of the Mughal rulers, monuments, and then the Surat Port where the British arrived as traders. The Gandhian era followed.

Since the country was under foreign rule we could not provide commentary. We satisfied ourselves with showing title cards and providing background music.

We discussed and finalised the last scene—we would conclude by highlighting the greatness of Gandhiji. Our friend from Poona, Trivedi, had given us the photograph of a postal envelope, sent from abroad, bearing the address:

Mahatma Gandhi
The King of India
New Delhi

We received several such photographs, but we included only a few of the significant ones. An important road in Bombay is called the Mahatma Gandhi Road. We photographed the postal cover on which Gandhiji himself had written 'Mahatma Gandhi Road'. This was on the cover addressed to a person living in that street. We filmed portraits of Gandhiji used by people for decorating their houses, offices and commercial undertakings. We recorded and choreographed the opinions of people like S. Radhakrishnan, Sir C.V. Raman, Romain Rolland and Dr. Maria Montessori. We tried to present the greatness of Gandhiji in our own way. It can be said that we succeeded to a great extent.

~

The world's largest film producers were the American company Kodak and the German Agfa. The branches of both these firms were in adjacent buildings on Hornby Road, in Bombay. The public relations officer of Agfa was the German-trained Dr. K.S. Hirlekar.

Due to the war, the import of films had been disrupted. The Agfa branch, as it belonged to the enemy country, came under the control of the British and therefore was closed down.

The Indian film producers had no alternative other than the Kodak Company. There were also the smaller firms: the British Ilford Selo, the Belgian Gewart and the Japanese Fuji.

Mistry, a middle-aged Parsi, was the distributor of Kodak films. He was a lean man with a stern face. But he was very kind; in fact, Dr. Pathy called him uncle.

Kodak sanctioned limits for their customers depending on their financial status. The limits ranged from Rs 1000 to Rs 50,000. Purchases could be done within the limit and the payments had to be made before the end of the succeeding month.

For two or three months I wrote cheques and bought films. Then I requested uncle to sanction me a limit of Rs 1000. He said, "You are a Chettiar. Chettiar means rich man. Buy the film and pay the money as usual."

How could he know that all Chettiars were not rich?

I was unhappy that I was not sanctioned a limit. I was angry too. I began buying a mild-coloured film called Light Amber from Ilford Selo. It was sufficient for regular use.

I bought about sixty thousand feet of film from Ilford Selo. Since I made cash purchase, I was allowed a five per cent discount. One day, the manager said to me, "If you buy one lakh feet of film, we can give an extra five per cent discount. But we cannot give that discount to a company. It will have to be credited to your personal account."

I said, "Give it to the company or don't give it at all."

The manager explained his inability, "This discount is given only to independent cinematographers. Our company policy does not permit us to do otherwise." I wondered if I should accept the concession and credit it to the company's account.

But if I did that, there might be all kinds of questions from the auditors. The directors and shareholders might think that I was getting a hefty discount and passing on only a part of it to the company.

I understood the value of Gandhiji's statement, 'Means justify the end.' I decided not to covet gain that accrued through wrong means.

After this incident I did not feel inclined to buy film from Ilford Selo.

I went to Kodak again and bought 5000 feet of film. When I was about to write the cheque, Mistry uncle noticed the counterfoils of the cheques drawn in favour of Ilford Selo.

He shouted at me, "Why have you thrown away so much money buying film from that company?"

"What else can I do? Didn't you refuse to give me any limit?"

He took out a printed form immediately, wrote down Rs 2500, and asked me to sign it.

In those days, Rs 2500 was a big amount. For that kind of money, one could buy 50,000 feet of positive film or 18,000 feet of negative film.

Kodak recognised only rich producers who invested money in lakhs and produced films in studios. The recognition accorded by Kodak to our modest documentary film company pleased us immensely. It also gained us a certain status in the film world.

~

We made an agreement with Wadia Movietone, one of the oldest studios in Bombay, to do the sound recording. We were to work for fifteen days at a daily rent of Rs 200. We could use one of the studio movieolas. The music director of the studio would provide mood music for our film. We did not have to pay laboratory charges for the film used by us. Besides being provided all these advantages, we were not charged when we exceeded the time limit by three days. The chairman, J.B.H. Wadia, was very proud that a film on Gandhiji was being produced in his studio. The kind cooperation extended by the studio personnel cannot be forgotten. Nor can we forget the interest shown by every studio worker in the production of the film.

~

We worked day and night for a week and somehow completed the editing of the film. The film was about Gandhiji and the history of the independence movement. We were very particular that there should be no room for any error.

K.M. Munshi, a Gujarati, and K.F. Nariman, a Parsi, were the most popular Congress leaders in Bombay. In 1937, when the Congress came to power in Bombay, there was a stiff fight between the two for prime ministership. Since the issue could not be settled between the two, a third candidate was chosen. He was Bal Gangadhar Kher, known as B.G. Kher, a modest young lawyer.

B.G. Kher was simple in his appearance. He was an earnest sympathiser of the poor, and was also a Gandhian. It is said that the then governor of Bombay, an Englishman, had a board hung in Kher's bedroom carrying the legend: 'I am the Prime Minister of Bombay Province.' John Gunther, an American writer, narrates this in his book *Inside Asia.*

During the war, the Congress ministry resigned and B.G. Kher was living in Khar. I told him that the cutting-copy of our film was ready and invited him to watch it and give us his opinion. He agreed to my request.

I made arrangements for a 9 a.m. screening at Broadway Talkies in Dadar. Kher and his wife arrived punctually. Having heard about his arrival, people had lined up on both sides of the road to pay their respects.

Since the commentary had not been recorded I stood beside him and explained the sequence.

While watching the funeral of Bal Gangadhar Tilak, Kher broke down. However, he checked his grief and told me that he too had been present in Tilak's funeral procession. Later, I came to know that they were relatives.

Kher told us that the editing of the film was flawless.

The film was released in Tamilnadu on 23 August 1940. I wrote a letter to Kher and got the following reply:

> I was very pleased to see the film of Mahatma Gandhi's life under production. I was deeply impressed by the difficulties in your way and the magnitude of your efforts in collecting the different news-reels from all over the world, and the result of your labour is indeed remarkable. I congratulate you on the production of your film.

Bal Gangadhar Kher was a true Gandhian.

I was not satisfied with showing the cutting-copy to just one person. So I approached the patriot Dr. Jivraj Mehta who was then very popular in Bombay.

Dr. Jivraj Mehta was one of the eminent physicians of India. He had suffered imprisonment for the nation's sake. His wife, Hansa Mehta, also a patriot, had courted arrest several times. Dr. Mehta had served as the prime minister of the Gujarat Province.

Dr. Mehta asked several questions while watching the cutting-copy. Since there was no recorded commentary I stood near him and explained what was happening. I drew his attention to Sapru. I pronounced the name Sapru as 'Saapru'.

Immediately, he shot back, "Why can't you learn to pronounce the names correctly?"

I did not understand what he was saying. He said, "'Sapru' not 'Saapru'".

I said, "I have been reading Tamil newspapers for twenty-five years. It is not easy to correct my pronunciation."

The Gandhi devotee Dr. Jivraj Mehta also said that the editing of the film was all right.

~

I felt that though the cutting-copy had been shown to political leaders, we ought to have some journalists watch it. Baburao Patel, editor of *Film India*, and K. Ahmad Abbas, assistant editor of the *Bombay Chronicle*, saw it. Along with them was my old friend from Hollywood, Ram Bagai.

K.A. Abbas made a few constructive suggestions. Abbas also wrote an excellent article in *Film India*, titled "Mahatma Gandhi Becomes a Film Star". I provided the material for the text, but it was Baburao Patel who gave the title. Neither Abbas nor I liked the title.

Patel did not stop with this. He gave a two-column, two-inch advertisement for the article in the *Times of India*.

The advertisement proclaimed: 'Mahatma Gandhi Becomes a Film Star'. It was a two-colour advertisement with the word 'Becomes' in red—as though ink had been spilt on it.

It was a second-rate advertisement that would create a wrong impression about Gandhiji. I am still unable to understand how a responsible publisher like the *Times of India* could issue such a cheap advertisement.

The very same day, I severed my connections with Baburao Patel, who had subjected a venerable topic to a crass commercial advertisement.

~

We bought the rights for Namakkal Ramalingam Pillai's songs *Aadu Raate* and *Kathiyinri Rathaminri,* but only used the former.

I met D.K. Pattammal's father and sought his permission for her to sing *Aadu Raate* for our film. I told him that due to financial constraints we could pay only a small amount. But I assured him that Pattammal would get a share in the royalty from the sale of gramophone records. He kindly agreed to let her sing for the film.

He died before the film was completed. In an article in *Ananda Vikatan* on Pattammal's father, Kalki mentions our meeting. Pattammal's father had told Kalki, "Chettiar came to meet me. He told me that it would be possible for them to pay only a small amount. Since it was for a film on Gandhi I readily agreed."

Pattammal's song suited the film splendidly. I think *Aadu Raate* was her only playback song.

After the editing was over, we began synchronising the playback songs with the music. We used Pattammal's song for the charka scene. When it was screened, many of the studio workers stopped their work and came to watch it.

The director of the famous Poddar Company, Mattur Subba Rao, who was like a father to us, was with us at that time. He was very glad that we were making good progress.

Excitement had been generated—an indicator of the film's success.

~

T. Suryakumari sang the song *Paadave Raatinamaam* for the charka scene in the Telugu version. She was the daughter of the brother of Andhra Kesari T. Prakasam, former premier of the Madras Province.

Chittoor V. Nagaiah and Bezwada Kumari Rajarathinam together sang the title song *Vande Mataram*.

Chittoor Nagaiah was not only a great actor but a fine human being as well. It is very rare for good actors to be good human beings. Nagaiah was an exception.

Bezwada Rajarathinam's song was used for the Sevagram scene.

The musician T.K. Jayarama Iyer asked his eldest daughter Chellammal to sing a song in praise of the greatness of Gandhiji for the conclusion of the Tamil version. She was a college student then. She, who sang under the pseudonym Dharmambal, later became the principal of Sarada College, Salem.

The scenes showing Gandhiji in England and Europe were about a thousand five hundred feet long. We decided to have western music for these scenes.

We sought the help of the popular Mehli Mehta, who was then playing violin in the orchestra of the internationally renowned Hotel Taj Mahal. Mehta was an honest and virtuous man. First he saw the film and noted down the duration of every scene. The 'fade in' and 'fade out' of music for each scene must be soft and pleasing to the ear. For this, it is customary to use mechanical devices. But Mehli Mehta said, 'Don't worry. I will adjust my playing accordingly, and begin and close the music in synchronisation with the scenes.'

Without ever looking at the clock, he stayed through the whole night and cooperated with us very kindly.

When he took leave of us, I put Rs 150 in an envelope and gave it to him. He immediately put it in his pocket.

"Please count the money," I said.

"I do not associate with such people," he said affectionately, and left.

One night, we were recording the music of the Wadia Movietone's orchestra. Since I had had a hectic day, I fell asleep.

Dr. Pathy woke me up and said, "Go home and get some rest. Otherwise your snoring will spoil our recording today."

The next day, when we developed the film, my snoring was heard over fifty feet of film—I felt so ashamed!

At this juncture an unexpected calamity befell us.

One morning, when we were discussing the day's work, a French man who was Dr. Pathy's friend, telephoned him from Delhi. He said that the officers of the news division of the then government in New Delhi were planning to seize the Gandhi film and destroy it. On hearing this warning we felt utterly paralysed.

At once, I decided to prepare six master copies of the film – which was still under production – and despatch them immediately to Chennai, and have them hidden in different places.

Normally, only one master positive is taken for a film. In the event of the negative getting damaged, more negatives could be made from the master positive. This is a precautionary measure. The cost of a master positive and an ordinary positive is almost the same. But a master positive cannot be used for screening in theatres. It is meant only for taking negatives.

I went to the Kodak firm and bought sixty thousand feet of master positive film. No producer would need or buy so much master positive film. For many years I was called 'Mr. Master Positive' in the Bombay Kodak Company circle.

First, we produced two copies. Instead of using our car, I hired a taxi and took them to Mattur Subba Rao's house in Santa Cruz. Over the next two days two more copies were produced. I placed them too in Subba Rao's hands. I entrusted two copies with my assistant and asked him to take them to our director in Chennai by train, travelling second class. I instructed him to tell the director to keep them hidden somewhere and not to disclose the details even to us.

All the six copies were finally taken to Chennai.

The political scene was in great turmoil. In such a situation, the brave and patriotic manner in which Mattur Subba Rao rendered help, unmindful of consequences, can never be forgotten.

Only after the war was over did I come to know that one copy was hidden in the palace of a native state, one in a mutt adjacent to a big temple and the others in the houses of different individuals.

I was tormented day and night by the fear that our Gandhi film, the nation's treasure, might be seized and that our labour of many years might be lost in a moment.

Even now I tremble in fear when I recollect those dark days.

Though it involved a huge, unexpected expenditure and a week's work, without a moment's rest, there was the consolation that all the six copies had reached Chennai safely.

God saved us from this terrible trial.

9

With the background music ready, we turned our attention to the commentary for the film. Under foreign rule, it is not possible to have a stirring commentary for a film promoting patriotism. Sometimes, silence can in fact yield better results.

For a two-and-a-half hour film, a single narrating voice, however pleasant, would prove monotonous. In those days, in America, they had initiated the fashion of narrating commentary using more than one voice (the multi-voice system) even for documentaries of ten minutes duration. Glam McCarthy's commentary for horse races was very famous. His narration would be as fast as a horse's gallop. Lowell Thomas was another reputed commentator. He became so popular that they produced a film titled *Going to Places with Lowell Thomas.*

Commentary writing and narrating were new to our country. I wanted to have four commentators; three men and one woman, and among the men, a 'star commentator'.

I consulted B.V. Acharya of All India Radio, Chennai, about the selection process. He suggested the name of S. Satyamurti, the Congress leader. I knew of him, but had no acquaintance with him. He was then the mayor of Chennai.

Satyamurti received me warmly. He had read some newspaper articles about the production of the Gandhi film. I asked him if he could read the commentary for specific scenes. I told him that we could pay him only five hundred rupees apart from meeting first-class fare for his travel to Bombay and back, and other incidental expenses.

He replied, "I am going to Bombay in a few days and will stay there for a couple of days. If you can give me my portion of the script, we can finish the work. But I will refer to the Mahatma only the way I do in public meetings. You need not pay for my travel and lodging. Instead, pay me a thousand rupees, as I have no other income." I was stunned to hear a leader of his stature telling me that he had no other income and that it would be better if I paid him a thousand rupees.

Though the amount demanded by him was a little steep, I agreed as I thought his commentary would enhance the value of the film.

No doubt it was our good luck that Satyamurti agreed to provide commentary. And it is a satisfying experience to talk about one's luck to others.

At that time, a Congress meeting was being held in Chennai. One of the directors of Documentary Films Limited had come to attend it. When I went to meet him, I found another Congress leader with him. I knew him too.

I proudly announced that Satyamurti had agreed to narrate the commentary and that I had agreed to pay Rs 1000 as he had requested.

Immediately, the popular Congress leader jumped to his feet and shouted, "What! A thousand rupees for Satyamurti! Atrocious! Should he charge any fee at all for a film on Gandhiji?" Our director nodded his head in approval.

I argued that the additional expense would amount to only about two hundred rupees, but would greatly enhance the value of the film and therefore our income. I pleaded saying that I had given my word. But both of them refused to yield.

I had enough authority to pay Rs 1000 to Satyamurti. There would have been no problem, had I done it without seeking the director's permission. But if I were to do it after the director had raised his objection, it would spoil the prospects of the film. So I decided to bear this insult for the film's sake.

I went to Satyamurti's house, cringing in shame, "Our director has refused to permit me to pay you a thousand rupees."

He said, 'It doesn't matter.'

I could see that he was saddened. That was but natural. But at that time I did not understand the full intensity of his disappointment.

Two days later I travelled to Bombay by second class on a train. Satyamurti happened to be one of my fellow passengers. Coupes with just two berths were a feature of first-class travel. But they were rare in second class. Usually married couples or lovers travelled by these coupes. In fact, some people paid more for this facility in order to misuse it. Out of concern for a great leader, the railway clerk had allotted the lower berth in the coupe to Satyamurti. By sheer accident I had been allotted the upper berth.

I greeted Satyamurti. He acknowledged the greeting. Five or six Congress men had come to garland him and see him off.

The train would reach Bombay the next morning at 10 o'clock. What a wonderful opportunity for me! I could converse with him for twenty-six hours and learn so much.

You would not believe me, but he did not speak a single word to me till he got down at Bombay. Severe punishment from God meted out to me for not keeping my word!

In retrospect, I understood why that Congress leader had so vociferously objected to our paying a thousand rupees to Satyamurti. He was a rich man—a non-Brahmin in the guise of a nationalist.

Patriots born in rich families by accident – many of them incompetent – treating able, but poor, patriots with vindictive intolerance on account of their poverty was indeed distressing.

Had he so wished, Satyamurti could have earned in lakhs and lived a life of ease and comfort. He was a peerless orator. He had been a terror to Reisman, the finance member of the imperial legislative council.

The untiring electioneering of Satyamurti was one of the reasons for the Congress victory in Tamilnadu in the 1937 elections.

The late Satyamurti, a devotee of Gandhiji, had dedicated his boundless talents to the nation.

Preparing the commentary for the film posed a huge problem. At that time there was no capable person in Tamilnadu – perhaps in the whole of India – who could write commentaries for films. It was something very new to India.

Though I had no experience in writing commentaries, I had seen a number of films with commentaries and had some knowledge of how it should be written. But if I were to write it myself, I would not be able to perceive the shortcomings. So I decided to find somebody for the task and assist him.

We consulted friends and decided to ask Tha.Naa. Kumaraswamy, the Tamil writer and translator. He modestly protested that he had no experience in that field. I said, "Don't worry. This field is new to India. Nobody has any experience in it. Let's make an effort." He agreed to give it a trial.

He came to Bombay and stayed there for a month. He saw the film a few times, read the available biographies of Gandhiji carefully and made notes. And he remained with us until all the commentators finished their work. For short scenes, the commentary had to be brief without sacrificing effective communication. This had to be explained to the commentators.

Kumaraswamy's hard work, patience and affability were admirable. It is true that there was no verve in his commentary. But that was not his fault. It was the fault of the time and the circumstances under which he wrote the commentary. We were satisfied that we could do that much given the constraints of the prevailing political situation.

B.V. Acharya, besides recommending three of the four commentators, wrote to them individually and requested them to cooperate with us. I thanked him for that. The commentators he had recommended were: Serukalathoor Sama, the popular actor; T.K. Jayarama Iyer, the popular violinist; and Vai.Mu. Kothainayagi Ammal, novelist and editor of *Jaganmohini.*

The fourth person I chose was Karaikudi Saw. Ganesan.

I should have asked B.V. Acharya to recommend the fourth person too. Instead, I made the choice and had to suffer the consequences.

After acting in *Ambikapathy* as Kambar, Serukalathoor Sama was at the peak of his fame. He had announced that he was going to produce two films—*Raja Bratruhari* and *Shylock.* Since he intended to direct both the films and also play the lead roles, he was extremely busy.

I met him at Hotel Woodlands in Chennai. He received me cheerfully and agreed to come to Bombay with me, putting his work on hold.

T.K. Jayarama Iyer was a man of fine qualities. Though his mother tongue was Telugu, he spoke excellent Tamil. He too agreed to come to Bombay.

I met Kothainayagi Ammal, who had been editing and publishing *Jaganmohini* for several years from her house in Thiruvallikeni, in Chennai. She too accepted the offer enthusiastically and came to Bombay.

I had not known any of these three people earlier.

We paid the commentators only a small fee. We provided them interclass railway ticket, accommodation, food and an honorarium of Rs 150. All of them stayed in the National Hindu Hotel in Bombay Fort. The charges were three and a quarter rupees for a single bed, tea in the morning, and lunch and dinner. We hired a car to take them to the studio which was five miles away.

All of them were very well off and earned a lot in those days. Despite being strangers and hailing from different fields, they worked in harmony due to their patriotism. It was their devotion to Gandhiji that united them.

When they took leave of us, I presented each of them with a copy of Gandhiji's autobiography in English. They accepted it as though it were a treasure.

~

The nobility and grandeur that characterised Serukalathoor Sama's voice provided a quality of stern elegance to the film.

One day, seeing me typing a letter, Sama said, "Let me do it for you. I've worked as a typist in the Madras Cosmopolitan Club to ward off starvation. Isn't typing for the Mahatma a blessing?"

Kothainayagi Ammal considered voicing the narration for this film a saintly duty. We used her sweet voice for scenes in which women appeared in large numbers. At times she spoke very emotionally. The solitary female voice provided a thread of sweetness among the male voices.

T.K. Jayarama Iyer was always cheerful and jovial. On certain occasions we would work right through the night. At sunrise he would play the music appropriate for dawn and immerse us in a sea of joy.

He too had a sweet voice. He spoke beautifully and forcefully.

For some sections of the film we recorded his violin renderings.

I wanted to recompense him, "We invited you only for the narration. But on our request you have also made the film musically rich. Please accept our gift."

At once, Jayarama Iyer, with tears glistening in his eyes, joined his palms above his head and said, "This is my offering to the Mahatma." That exemplary man refused to accept anything.

⁂

I sent a telegram to Saw. Ganesan, who was then in Karaikudi. He presumed that he was the sole narrator and issued a press note to that effect in the weekly *Ooliyan* edited by Raya. Cho. A copy of the weekly reached us even before he reached Bombay.

Being an old friend, he stayed with us in our office.

In the studio, fifteen minutes after the audition, the sound engineer sent the note signed 'reject'. I felt thunderstruck on seeing it. We had brought him to Bombay from Karaikudi, and his hasty press note had already been published.

I could not engage him against the opinion of the sound engineer. Not only would it tell upon the quality of the film it would also bother my conscience. My colleagues too would lose faith in me. Not knowing what to do, I felt miserable.

I had committed a grievous error in choosing the fourth narrator without consulting my friend in All India Radio.

I had misjudged the suitability of Ganesan's loud voice. Our friendship, which can be traced to my Rangoon days, and my admiration for him had misled me.

But Dr. Pathy found a way out of our dilemma. He said, "In the numerous 'crowd scenes' the slogan *Mahatma Gandhikku Jai!* is prominent. We will ask Ganesan to speak when there are crowds and processions. That will not affect the film. We must not disappoint a person who has come such a long way."

I thanked God for the timely solution.

⁂

In life, happiness and sorrow alternate. We experienced this in full measure while producing the Gandhi film.

One morning, a middle-aged Englishman came to our office. He was on the editorial board of *Picturepost,* the most popular illustrated weekly published from London. It enjoyed wide readership in India, and he had come to India as its correspondent.

He said, "I returned from Wardha yesterday. I conversed with Mahatma Gandhi there. I happened to know about your documentary on Gandhiji from newspaper reports. I told Mahatma Gandhi about it and asked him 'Would you like to see your own film?' And the Mahatma replied, 'I am eagerly looking forward to see it.' I came just to deliver this good news."

Gandhiji saw films very rarely. And I had thought that he would never agree to see our documentary on him.

When I heard the words of Gandhiji through this person I felt as though Gandhiji was seeing our film at that very moment.

I was flooded by an indescribable joy.

10

In Bombay, we arranged a screening of the film for ourselves as soon as the first Tamil print was ready. We noticed some lapses, but in our overwhelming euphoria they seemed like trifles and were soon forgotten.

We did not call it the *Life History of Mahatma Gandhi*. Instead, we titled the film *Mahatma Gandhi: His Movements and Activities.*

When we screened it for our friends in Chennai, it received a royal welcome—mainly because the film exceeded everybody's expectations.

Most people had doubted whether a full-length film could be made, based on the events of Gandhiji's life. To be honest, we too had been apprehensive, though we did not advertise our uncertainty.

On the release of the first print, our dream had come true.

~

The film had to be censored in Chennai. The chairman of the censor board was the commissioner of police, an Englishman. The board consisted of twenty members, most of them nominated by the government. Some belonged to the Justice Party and some to the Muslim League, and there were none from the Congress. But there were a few nationalists.

Foreign rule. Wartime. A film showing the independence movement and its architect, Gandhiji. Furthermore, there were scenes showing brutal and despicable lathi charges by the police, and the non-violent struggle of men and women unknown to history. In addition, there were the whispers about the government's plan to confiscate the film. We were terribly anxious, and worried constantly whether the censor board would clear it for public viewing.

We went to the office of the commissioner of police and submitted the application. The officer who received the application was a Tamil. He understood our plight from the fear writ large on our faces and treated us kindly. He said, "Two members of the censor board will have to see the film. It is my prerogative to decide who they are. I will assign the work to members who'll be suitable for this task."

A patriot and Gandhi devotee in the office of the commissioner of police! We relaxed a little.

Fortunately, K. Srinivasan, the editor of the *Hindu*, and Dr. U. Krishna Rao were the members selected for certifying the film.

I knew *Hindu* Srinivasan a little. He was a patriot who wore only khadi.

Born in Mangalore, Dr. Krishna Rao had settled in Chennai. He belonged to the family of Dr. U. Rama Rao and many of his family members were well-known doctors. All of them participated in public activities and were patriots.

On the appointed day, both of them came to Paragon Talkies to see the film.

I sat next to Srinivasan and talked about general matters. When the lathi charge appeared on screen (for about three minutes), he asked me, "Did this really happen?" That was the only question he asked me regarding the film.

I said, "Yes. Everything you see in this film actually happened."

After the film was over, both of them arrived at their decision within a closed room and entrusted the recommendation to a police officer.

I was extremely eager to know the decision of the censor board members. But I did not have the courage to ask either of them. There was a fierce struggle between desire and fear in my palpitating heart, and fear won.

The next morning, our friend from All India Radio, B.V. Acharya, came and chided us in his usual manner, "Why are you moping about like lazy louts? Shouldn't you be attending to the film's release?"

I said, "The decision of the censor board has not been declared yet."

"Oh! You are worried about that. I will go and ask *Hindu* Srinivasan right away," he said and left in his car.

We were on tenterhooks awaiting his arrival. Acharya was back in ten minutes, yelling, "Passed in toto." To me, those words were like Hanuman's words to Rama on his return from Lanka: "I saw Sita."*

"When I went there, Srinivasan was having his bath," said Acharya. "So I shouted, 'What happened to the film?' He shouted back, 'Passed in toto.' Start your work immediately."

We thanked Acharya for his help.

~

This was the first time in world history that a foreign government had permitted the screening of a film detrimental to its interests. Mr. Hailes, the editor of the *Madras Mail* wrote, "The British government has permitted the screening of a film inimical to its interests. The British alone can do something like this." It is absolutely true. Once the censor board had passed the film, the government did not interfere with the decision.

What the British government did not contemplate, a Tamil did. When the film was released in Thiruvananthapuram, Sir C.P. Ramaswamy Iyer, then diwan of Travancore, ordered the excision of the police lathi-charge scene.

Later in 1953, when I met the same Sir C.P. Ramaswamy Iyer, at his behest, in San Francisco, he heard all about the film from me and said, with palms joined together, "Gandhi was a great soul. I will help in the production of your film in all possible ways."

~

The British government did not object to the decision of the censor board, but it did not forget the 'treason' of the two members either. Their term was not extended, as was common practice. This loss was their reward for passing the film on Gandhiji.

When I met Srinivasan, he said, "I was not nominated for the board again, but I have no regrets. I am happy that the Gandhi film was released."

---

* *'Kanden Seethayai'* (literally, 'I saw Sita') is a popular quote from the Tamil classic *Kambaramayanam.*

Likewise, Krishna Rao said, "They did not nominate me again. However, I am satisfied that I had the opportunity to permit the screening of the film."

Rajaji included Krishna Rao in the ministry he formed in 1952–53. On getting to know about it through the newspapers, I wrote a congratulatory letter from America. He thanked me by airmail. Though a minister, he had not used government service stamps. I have written letters to a large number of ministers. Most of them have replied, but only two of them did not use service stamps. One was Rajaji, and the other, Krishna Rao.

It was the patriotism of Srinivasan and Krishna Rao that enabled lakhs and lakhs of people to see the Gandhi film, that too, during wartime.

Advertisements can significantly influence the success of a film. Our film was lucky in that respect too. On the recommendation of a friend, we engaged a Chennai firm, Premier Advertising Service, to work on the publicity. We printed two lakh stamps featuring Gandhiji and distributed them among school children. The children proudly affixed them in their textbooks. We also produced a beautiful two-colour calendar with Gandhiji's picture and supplied them to commercial establishments. Even today, one can come across that lovely picture in some shops. We made a lot of posters of different types, folders in art paper, etc. Besides these, we made large photographs for display in studios and many types of blocks for newspapers.

But before we engaged an advertising firm, something interesting happened. A student from Tamilnadu, who had just finished his collegiate education, used to come to meet us when we were in Bombay. When we made arrangements to advertise in the front page of the *Hindu,* we entrusted this young man with the preparation of the text for the advertisement.

The correct titular description should have been 'The Documentary Film on Mahatma Gandhi'. But this person, thinking that he was smart, phrased it as 'Mahatma Gandhi in Celluloid'.

We failed to notice it and the advertisement was published.

A few days later, mistaking 'celluloid' for dolls made of celluloid, a lawyer from a city in Andhra Pradesh, wrote to us: "Please send one dozen by V.P.P."

~

In those days, film producers used to make twenty prints for a film and release them simultaneously in important towns. There was an advantage to this practice. Even if the film was bad, it would make a sizable collection well before the reviews reached the general public. We did not like this business tactic nor did we have the means to indulge in it.

Even the production of five prints was an uphill task for us. Our plan was to release it in Chennai and four other cities. Krishnamurthy, the younger brother of N.M.R. Subbaraman, met me in Poona while the film was still under production and told me that the film should be screened in their cinema theatre in Madurai, the famous Chintamani Talkies. He made all arrangements enthusiastically and also wished to screen the film in a theatre under their management in Tirunelveli. We agreed to his suggestion.

Most of the shareholders of Documentary Films Limited were from Chettinadu. So we made arrangements for screening the film in Karaikudi. In Coimbatore, the proprietor of a respectable theatre came forward to screen the film, and we agreed.

But in 'charitable' Chennai, no theatre-owner came forward. Some were indifferent; some were afraid. Reputed cinema journals published from Chennai and other parts of the country wrote that Chennai had been lagging behind in film production and that the Madras Presidency could now hold its head high with the production of the Gandhi film. Yet, nobody was willing to screen it. We even thought of bringing a touring cinema to the Island Grounds especially for screening this film.

A famous Parsi company owned several theatres in Bombay and a few other cities. They had taken a few theatres on annual lease in cities like Chennai. One of them was Roxy Theatre, where they screened only English films. The manager of that theatre came to our office one morning unexpectedly. He had a proposal, 'We wish to screen the film on the

Mahatma in our theatre for two weeks, make your own arrangements for the third week. We accept all your conditions. Your publicity is all right, though you can probably do something better for Chennai."

The film ran very successfully in Roxy for two weeks. I went there often. One day, I asked the manager, "How is it that you who only show English films came forward to screen our film?"

He replied, "We are now showing a Twentieth Century Films' production starring Shirley Temple. Though we would get a bonus if we increased the collections, I wrote to our head office in Bombay and sought their permission to suspend the Shirley Temple film and screen the Gandhi film.

"There is an important reason for this. In 1930, I was the manager of a theatre called Capital in Boribandar, Bombay. I was living with my family within the theatre compound. This was during the Salt Satyagraha—for several days the Bombay police lathi charged thousands of Congress volunteers. My sister kept weeping over this brutality. She is now living with me in Chennai. It's her repeated entreaty that led me to volunteer to screen the film on the Mahatma."

The unblemished patriotism of a Parsi woman was responsible for the screening of our film in one of the reputed cinema halls of Chennai.

At the same time, I must also mention the two Justice Party heavyweights who categorically refused to screen the Gandhi film 'on principle'. One was Rao Sahib M. Vedachala Mudaliar who was the chairman of the Chengalpattu Municipality for many years and who owned the only theatre in that town. The other was T. Sundararao Naidu, the former mayor of the Chennai Corporation. According to newspaper reports, he died in the common ward of the Royapettah Government Hospital.

We screened the Tamil version of the Gandhi film in Chennai and other important cities on 23 August 1940. I can never forget the fervent enthusiasm and the admirable patriotism shown by the press and also the substantial help given by them. Everyone looked upon the film as their own.

Many newspapers issued special Mahatma Gandhi film supplements on 17 August 1940. The usual practice was to demand two pages of advertisement for a four-page supplement. For us, they did not even insist on one page of advertisements. But we did not have any difficulty as the firms – His Master's Voice that distributed the musical records of the film and Sakthi that did the printing – provided advertisements for the supplement.

The English dailies *Indian Express* and *Free Press*; the Tamil dailies *Swadesamitran, Dinamani* and *Bharata Devi*; the English weeklies *Sunday Times, Free India* and *Modern Times*; and the Tamil weekly *Hindustan,* issued supplements. And most of the monthlies and weeklies published from Chennai carried Gandhiji's portrait on the cover.

In those days, *Dinamani* also published an evening daily with Va.Raa. as its editor. Under the instruction of T.S. Chokkalingam, the editor of *Dinamani,* Va.Raa. acquired details regarding the film and wrote an excellent article.

R.A. Padmanabhan, the assistant editor of *Hindustan,* evinced interest in the film right from the beginning. His special article was printed on the last pages of *Hindustan* and the *Sunday Times*. The English daily *Bombay Sentinel* published the *Sunday Times* article prominently—in bold type with large captions. Its editor Horniman, an Englishman, was banished from India for some time by the British government for his involvement in the Indian freedom struggle. K. Ahmad Abbas' articles published in the *Bombay Chronicle* also deserve to be mentioned here. I received complete information on the published materials, in connection with the release of the Gandhi film, only when I went to Ahmedabad a few years later.

~

We arranged a special show for the press before the release of the film. Almost all the editors sent their correspondents, and some even came in person. The editors of the Telugu and Urdu papers in Chennai, and the Chennai correspondents of popular journals in Malayalam, Kannada, Bengali, Gujarati, Marathi and Hindi also came to the show. *Veerakesari* of Colombo, *Burma Nadu* and *Jothi* of Rangoon, and *Tamil Nesan* of Kuala Lumpur showed special interest.

When the film was released in Chennai, I deliberately stayed away. Of course, I liked being praised by friends. But if they praised me in my presence, I would feel greatly embarrassed. To avoid this I went to Coimbatore.

In Coimbatore, I saw the film along with T.A. Ramalingam Chettiar, a famous lawyer and a member of the legislative assembly. T.S. Avinashilingam Chettiar was his nephew. Ramalingam Chettiar had ably developed the cooperative movement in Coimbatore. He enjoyed the film and congratulated me affectionately.

Next morning, I reached Chennai. A director of our company came to receive me at the Chennai Central station. M. Satyanarayana, the secretary of Hindi Prachar Sabha, congratulated us the moment he saw us, and said, "You have successfully countered the stay order."

Puzzled, I queried the director. He clarified Satyanarayana's comment, "A young man came to our office on the morning of 22 August and sent word to meet me, 'I want to meet him on a very important matter. If he doesn't meet me now he will regret it greatly.' I asked him to come to my room immediately. He was a lawyer, and he had come straight from the court. He said, 'A stay order has been obtained against your film. I came to inform you.' I was aghast. Fortunately, he had noted down the reason for the stay order. Somebody had pleaded stating that the portion of the film depicting Gandhiji's journey to London from Bombay was his property.

"Immediately, I went through our records and found a payment receipt for this shot and a letter authorising us to use it as we desired. I engaged a good lawyer at once and handed over all the records to him. The next morning the order was withdrawn. I decided not to alarm you, but wait till you reach Chennai to inform you about this."

The film clipping of Gandhiji travelling from Bombay to London was one hundred and fifty feet long. Of that, we used about a hundred feet. The man who obtained the stay order by giving a false statement that he was the owner of a hundred feet of film in the documentary of twelve thousand feet was Avudaiappa Chettiar.

Avudaiappa Chettiar was known for his daring exploits as a pilot. And he was daring in other kinds of nefarious activities too. The stay order was one such endeavour.

The cinema industry came to know about Avudaiappa Chettiar's case. A representative of the Bombay firm that sold us this shot met us. He said that Avudaiappa Chettiar had got this shot from them a few years ago, but had not paid for it and had refused to return the negative in spite of repeated letters. They had sold it to us much later. He added that cheats like Avudaiappa Chettiar should be punished severely and that they were ready to join us and fight him legally.

The case came up for enquiry a few days later. The judge not only dismissed the case but also ordered Avudaiappa Chettiar to pay the costs.

Documentary Films Limited, the company that produced the Gandhi film, was a private limited company. There were fifty shareholders, of whom forty-six were Nattukkottai Chettiars. Most of them had invested not for the profit, but because they were convinced that it was a good cause.

To get a stay order when the film was about to be released was an inhuman act. We had produced this film on Gandhiji, the architect of our freedom and the Father of our Nation, in the face of innumerable difficulties, when an alien nation was ruling our country and during wartime. The man who committed this heinous sin of filing a false and despicable case against us without any reason or justification was also a Nattukkottai Chettiar!

It was the patriotism of that young lawyer from Mylapore that had protected us from that last-minute disaster.

~

On the day the film was released in Karaikudi, Dr. Alagappa Chettiar, Raya. Cho. and others saw the film. Nawab Rajamanickam was staging plays in the nearby town Devakottai. He suspended the performance of his play and brought his entire troupe to see the film on the first day. Afterwards, as long as the film was being shown to the public in Karaikudi, he recommended it to his audience at every drama performance.

The *Hindu* reported that the first show in Chennai was witnessed by V.S. Srinivasa Sastri, T.R. Venkatrama Sastri and G.A. Natesan, and that the latter two could see themselves in the scene showing the 1928 Calcutta All Party Conference.

The Congress leaders Kamaraj Nadar, Omandur Ramasamy Reddiar and others saw the film buying second-class tickets.

One day, I saw Diwan Bahadur A.M.M. Murugappa Chettiar watching the film from the balcony.

On one Saturday, the students of the Stanley Medical College reserved the entire balcony to see the film.

T.S. Avinashilingam Chettiar brought four sanyasis to see the film with the permission of the head of the Ramakrishna Mutt.

A couple who had come to see the film from a nearby village waited in the theatre for three hours and saw the 9.30 show as they could not get tickets for the 6.30 show.

The Gandhi film had the unique honour of attracting people from all walks of life.

~

I invited Rajaji to see the film. He said that he would come for the 6.30 show and that he did not need a car or an escort.

Punctuality was one of Rajaji's admirable traits. He arrived alone at the appointed time, in a friend's car. I took him through the lounge of the theatre. The theatre workers had aesthetically displayed a number of large photographs connected with the Gandhi film, supplements issued by journals, and cover photographs of Gandhiji from about thirty magazines.

Rajaji observed all these very keenly and asked me, "What did you do to get Gandhiji's picture printed in all these magazines at the same time?" I did not answer him.

The Gandhi film was twelve thousand feet long. In those days, Tamil films ranged from eighteen thousand to twenty thousand feet. English films were shorter, but they showed some trailers in the beginning. I considered making a trailer of about one thousand five hundred feet, but gave up the idea due to paucity of funds.

So, I bought stock shots on wars at cheap prices from foreign companies in Bombay, did a little editing and showed them as a supporting programme with Tamil commentary before the start of the film.

The war sequence provoked someone to ask a legitimate question, "Is it appropriate to show this war shot along with the film on the apostle of non-violence?"

I wriggled out of the situation by employing a stock reply, "Only if people see the horrors of war would they understand the significance of non-violence." But the truth was, the exigencies of the situation had caused me to unthinkingly commit a folly.

I took Rajaji to the balcony. I feared what Rajaji might have to say on seeing the war sequence. Fortunately, by the time we reached our seats, it had come to a close and the film had started.

Because the lights had been dimmed, even those who were in the balcony did not notice the arrival of Rajaji. I found a comfortable seat for him. I preferred to stand a little away when eminent men watched the film. If necessary, I would sit behind them, and only for a little while.

During the interval, the lights were turned on. People in the balcony noticed Rajaji. There was some commotion and the news reached others. The slogan '*Rajajikku Jai*' was raised and a boisterous demonstration followed. It took some time to subside. Spectators were immensely happy that they were seeing the film on Gandhiji with Rajaji.

During the interval, I went up to him and asked, "May I get you a cup of hot coffee?" A north Indian journalist had once written, "Rajaji would be mighty pleased if the entire river Kaveri were to run with coffee."

But Rajaji said, "Bring me a cold drink." Perhaps if I had asked him what he wanted he might have asked for a cup of coffee.

Rajaji was an impeccable guest. This was another of his extraordinary traits. Most political leaders would not keep time, they would make us wait with a car or would bring a battalion along with them. Among them, some would indulge in all kinds of mischief. Some would order us about. Only if one had experienced such behaviour could one truly appreciate Rajaji.

After the interval, Rajaji too appeared in certain scenes. At such times there was no limit to the joyous outcries of the audience. This show of jubilation continued till the end.

After the show was over I led Rajaji to his car. Hundreds of people surrounded the car. Press correspondents put questions to him. The car left amidst slogans hailing him.

I read what Rajaji had to say about the film in *Free India* that week. "I never expected it to be so good. It is well done."

It is not easy to get a good chit from Rajaji, the man whom Gandhiji had praised as 'the guardian of my conscience'.

~

One day, when I was in Roxy theatre, there was a telegram for me from Bombay. It was from K. Gopalaswamy, one of the managing editors of the *Times of India.* He was from Tamilnadu and he wrote good English. I knew him fairly well. He was also the sole Indian representative of the famous Associated Press of America.

I read the telegram. I read it again and again. As I read, my head swelled with pride. The message was: "America enquires when you are leaving."

Why would I not gloat with pride when America, the land of abundance, beckoned a commoner like me?

But slowly and surely I realised that America had enquired not about me but my holy task of tracking the Mahatma on film.

Mass-spinning scene from the film

A.K. Chettiar with Romain Rolland and his sister
(from *Sakti*, February 1945)

Publicity material 1

டாக்குமெண்டரி பிலிமில்
தரிசனம் அளிக்கும்

மகாத்மா காந்தி

Publicity material 2

APPENDIX

Appendix 1

At midnight, 14 August 1947, India achieved complete independence. The British, who had ruled India for centuries, handed over power to the representatives of the Indian nation in a peaceful manner.

Bharati's dream of liberty for everybody had materialised.

Only those who had suffered the miserable agony of foreign rule, at least for a few years, and had made some sacrifice for the nation, could appreciate the value of freedom.

The Constituent Assembly of India met on the midnight of 14 August in New Delhi. Most of its members were venerable patriots.

At midnight, when the proceedings of the Assembly were about to begin, a man seated in the last row got up and shouted *'Mahatma Gandhi ki Jai'*. All present echoed the cry. At that moment, only one person occupied the heart of every Indian! He was the Mahatma who had risen to revive this country from its state of ruination.

Lord Mountbatten, who had been the viceroy until the previous day, took over as the first governor-general of India—an unparalleled example of the courtesy and generosity of Indians.

On the evening of 15 August, Lord Mountbatten hoisted the Indian national flag and saluted it. This, in turn, was an example of English courtesy and generosity.

Undoubtedly a rare happening in the entire history of the world.

I was one of the lakhs of Indians who had enjoyed witnessing this remarkable event.

~

We had released our film on the life of Gandhiji in 1940 with Tamil and Telugu commentaries, in succession. Afterwards, fearing confiscation by the British government due to the turbulent political situation, we hid the copies of the film in temples, religious mutts and the residences of friends. When India was about to gain independence, I strongly wished for the film to be screened for the venerable gathering of patriots in New Delhi. I did not have any idea about how it could be done. But, with the help of friends, I decided to leave for New Delhi by air, with the film box in tow.

In those days, the Tata firm ran the civil air services. Their Chennai office was located in Khaleel Mansion on Mount Road. There were no fast planes. If one left Chennai in the morning, one could reach Delhi only by evening.

The person in charge said that all flights were heavily booked due to independence day celebrations. When I explained my predicament, he suggested that I leave for Bombay that very evening and take a flight to Delhi from there. I bought my tickets immediately.

While I was buying the tickets, the proprietor of a famous hotel in Chennai whom I knew, kept looking at me intently.

He finally approached me, "Chettiar, I have never travelled by an airplane. Do you think it is safe to travel by air?" I assured him that he could travel without any fear. I can still recall the look of fear on his face.

I reached Bombay that evening by the specified flight. Those of us who were proceeding to Delhi from there were hosted by the airport authorities at Hotel Taj Mahal. They had also arranged for us to be taken to the airport the next day. We reached Delhi within a few hours.

From the airport, I went to my friend's house in Connaught Circus. I spent sometime there and left for the *Hindustan Times* office. I requested K. Santhanam, who worked there, to help me.

Santhanam, without evincing any interest, said, "Everybody is involved in the independence day celebrations. Who will come to see your film now? After the celebrations are over we'll screen the film in some theatre. We can seek the help of the members of the South India Club."

I came out feeling dejected. There were only four days left for independence. I wandered around Connaught Circus not knowing what to do.

I saw the name R. Chakravarthy, M.A., B.L. listed on the board of the Traffics Insurance Company. I knew Chakravarthy, but not very well. He had moved to Delhi as the representative of the Seshasayee Company only a few months earlier.

Chakravarthy received me kindly. When I explained my problem to him, he enthusiastically provided me with the services of two young men employed in his company, a servant, a telephone and a car for this holy work.

We then chalked out a plan. First, a cinema hall was to be fixed. There were only four cinema halls in New Delhi and all of them were situated in Connaught Place. Chakravarthy took me to Rajeshwar Dayal, the proprietor of Regal Theatre.

Dayal's response was jubilant, "It is my fortune that you ask me when there are so many other halls available. I'll pull out whatever film is being screened and also bear all the expenses. But I have a request—my family and I must be permitted to see the film. It is enough even if we get some space to stand."

The first task was completed. Then, I went to the house of Babu Rajendra Prasad, the president of the Constituent Assembly, to request him to preside over the function. I met Anand Mohan Sahay by chance at Rajendra Prasad's house.

Sahay was a Bihari. Earlier, he had been Rajendra Prasad's secretary. He was married to the daughter of the excellent national service volunteer Urmila Devi, who was the sister of the Bengali leader C.R. Das. Sahay had lived in Japan for many years where he established a branch of the Indian National Congress and also a hostel named 'India Lodge'. He helped Indians in general and students in particular. I was one among those Indian students who had had their education under his benign and strict supervision. He had been like a father to all of us.

Sahay was very pleased to see me. When I explained the purpose of my visit, he said, "Rajan Babu is taking rest, so come at six in the evening. I will speak to him and make the necessary arrangements."

I went there on time. Rajan Babu was seated in a chair on the lawn, surrounded by many assistants. Sahay introduced me to him. I requested him to preside over the screening of the Gandhi film.

Rajan Babu conversed cheerfully. He asked me, "Do you know why everyone is joining the Congress nowadays?" And he provided the answer himself, "In those days joining the Congress meant misery, poverty and sacrifice, and nothing else. But today you stand to gain in every way. That's why a lot of people are joining the Congress now."

People standing near him objected loudly to his attending the film show. They said that he had to attend the Assembly at midnight and that his health would suffer. Rajan Babu asked for his engagement diary and made an entry under the date 14 August: "6 p.m. to 8 p.m. Mahatma Gandhi Film, Regal Cinema". I took leave of him respectfully. After my meeting with Rajan Babu, I came out with a solemn feeling, as though I had visited a temple.

Sahay then took me inside Rajan Babu's house. He telephoned Pandit Jawaharlal Nehru and tried to persuade him to attend the screening. But Nehru expressed his inability due to prior engagements and said that he would send his daughter Indira instead. And he sent her as promised.

I met Chakravarthy again and narrated all that had happened. The second task was the printing of the invitations. We did it the same night.

With Chakravarthy, I went to the office of the Constituent Assembly and got the addresses of all the Assembly members. We also collected the addresses of all the consulates in Delhi. From the Press Information Bureau we got the addresses of all the foreign correspondents. We met the president of the Association of Indian press correspondents, Durga Das, who was also the managing editor of the *Hindustan Times.* He took fifty invitations from us saying that he would deliver them himself. The young men from Chakravarthy's office worked untiringly.

We met R.K. Shanmukham Chettiar who had by then been nominated the first finance minister of free India. He said affectionately, "You have come such a long way from our place and you are doing such commendable work. I will definitely come for the screening."

We went to the Press Trust of India and met its manager, Sir Ushanath Sen. An experienced administrator, he readily agreed to despatch the information to all the newspapers.

We then met a young officer at the All India Radio. He said zestfully, "I will broadcast this news in seven languages."

After these visits, wherever I went, I began receiving phone calls from unexpected quarters. Most of the calls came to Regal Theatre. I received a call even when we were in Rajan Babu's house to give him the invitation. The caller said, "I am Patel. Don't you remember me? I'm the President of the Association of Indians. I have come to attend the independence celebrations. I earnestly request you to give me an invitation for the screening of the film on Gandhi."

At Regal Theatre I received a call, and the speaker said, "I am Mrs. R.K. Nehru. I'll be grateful if you could give me an invitation. Congratulations."

We sent invitations to all those who made such requests. Due to lack of time, we made arrangements for personal delivery.

Chakravarthy and I went to invite Santhanam.

We sent an invitation through Rama Seshadri, on his request, to his friend Major General Himmat Singh.

All the morning papers of 14 August carried news about the screening of the Gandhi film. The All India Radio announced it repeatedly.

Rajeshwar Dayal had arranged for Regal Theatre to be decorated very beautifully.

Right from the morning, people began thronging the theatre. They begged for invitations. The telephone kept ringing all the while. People were extremely eager to see the film.

Guests began arriving from 5 o'clock onwards. Many young men served as volunteers. A middle-aged man in khaki shorts and a white shirt came up to me, shook hands and introduced himself, "My name is Hardikar." I was amazed. He was Dr. Hardikar, the eminent patriot educated in America. I had heard a lot about him in India and America. He belonged to Belgaum. He had founded a national service corps called the Hindustan Seva Dal and was managing it very ably.

On independence day, since celebrations had been organised everywhere, be it a village or a town or a city, most of the national leaders had stayed in their own native places. Patriotic Indians from every nook and corner of the country converged in New Delhi. Many noteworthy persons among them came to see the film. Devadas Gandhi, the son of Gandhiji, also came.

Ambassadors of foreign countries, local and foreign correspondents, members of the legislature and all the chief guests arrived before the appointed time.

As in mammoth weddings, many came uninvited. The seats were full. Many sat on the floor and in the aisles. More than a hundred were standing. In the jubilant euphoria of independence nobody cared for nor insisted on regulations.

The show began exactly at six. Since the film had not been screened for several years a lot of restoration had to be done. Of the twelve reels, ten were in Tamil and two in Telugu. Not even ten per cent of the audience knew these two languages. But everybody was aware of Gandhiji's life. So the language of the commentary was not a problem.

Babu Rajendra Prasad came with his family. The audience in the hall stood up in respect.

When Gandhiji appeared for the first time in the film there was continuous applause and happy cheering. Though at that time Gandhiji was in Calcutta, he was in everybody's heart.

Many felt a sense of deprivation as Gandhiji, the architect of India's freedom and the Father of the Nation, was not present in the capital that day.

Hundreds of patriots appeared in the film. Some in the audience saw themselves on the screen. Patriots in hundreds for whom the country's freedom had been their very breath and who had sacrificed their lives and souls to the nation came back to life. Rightly, the show turned out to be a homage to them.

This was the first time that a show had been arranged for a venerable gathering of supreme patriots from all over the country.

The show ended exactly at eight. I met all those who had helped me and expressed my gratitude individually. After a light dinner I dozed off.

I woke up around midnight and rushed to Connaught Place. There were innumerable loudspeakers and hundreds of people standing in front of them. The bazaars, streets, parks—all were decorated beautifully. What a huge display of coloured lights! And national flags! And festoons!

The Assembly was called to order at midnight. The alien British government handed over the Indians their liberty—their birthright. They transferred the rights and powers to the elected representatives of the Indians.

The renowned commentator De Mello described the day's programmes over the radio. I was very eager to listen to everything. But sleep was overpowering me, so I listened to him in snatches.

The next day, Major General Himmat Singh came to Rama Seshadri's house. He was the younger brother of the Maharaja of Jam Nagar in Saurashtra. He thanked me for the invitation to the film show and said, "As a token of my gratitude, I give you this."

It was an invitation for the flag-hoisting ceremony by Lord Mountbatten that evening. With that invitation I could sit comfortably in the first row among the VIPs and watch the ceremony

I went an hour ahead of time and sat there very proudly. My pride did not last for long. In half an hour, the crowd became so uncontrollably large that I stood on my chair and prayed to God that I should not get crushed in the melee.

The midnight programme of 14 August 1947 was for the representatives of India. But the 15 August programme was for the public.

Lakhs of people were sitting in a vast maidan; only a small area around the flagpole was vacant. The flood of jubilation eclipsed the flood of humanity. Bharati's song "Oh! See our motherland's beautiful flag" came to my mind. A little later, two Punjabi youths walked into the ring formed by the people with a portrait of Netaji Subash Chandra Bose. The joyous and excited applause of the people could very well be described as 'sky splitting'.

As the appointed time drew near, the crowd swelled. People surged around the flagpole. With great difficulty Lord Mountbatten and Prime Minister Jawaharlal Nehru found their way to the dais. Due to tumultuous uproar and chaos, they could not adhere to the programme. Yet, at the fixed moment, Mountbatten hoisted the national flag of free India and saluted. The same moment a rainbow appeared in the sky. People welcomed it as a good augury. With great difficulty the police escorted Mountbatten and Nehru out of the crowd.

The next morning, my friends saw me off at the Delhi railway station. It was a holiday for all sections except the ticket counter, so the film box could not be weighed and charged. I kept it underneath the berth in my second-class compartment.

The Delhi–Chennai Grand Trunk Express, the fastest train in those days, took 52 hours to reach Chennai.

In all the stations on the way, the independence day decorations remained more or less intact.

On the third morning, I reached Chennai Central. I handed over the film box to one of the porters who had mobbed me and directed him to take it to the taxi stand. A young railway officer demanded the luggage receipt for the film box. I said, "I don't have it." At once, in an officious manner, he ordered the porter to take the box to the weighing machine. I followed them.

I explained to the railway officer that the day I left Delhi had been a holiday for the luggage-booking office, and that I had no intention of cheating the railways. I mentioned that the box contained reels of the film on Mahatma Gandhi and that I had taken it to New Delhi for screening it during the independence day celebrations.

The officer's face changed. He stood stunned and was unable to say anything. He then asked me, "Why didn't you mention this earlier?" and ordered the porter to take it to the taxi stand. He accompanied us up to the taxi.

The porter placed the box inside the luggage compartment. I tried to pay the porter, but he stubbornly refused to accept any money despite my insistence.

The taxi started. The porter and the officer saw me off.

I was happy that I had been blessed with the boon of producing the film on Mahatma Gandhi. Though I did not show it, I felt proud about it. At times, I felt that I was reasonably justified in taking pride in myself.

But when a porter, belonging to the kind that would never be satisfied with whatever amount you might pay, refused to accept his legitimate wage due to his devotion towards Gandhiji, I bowed my head in shame.

"Sudanthira Dina Ninaivugal"
April 1978, *Kumari Malar*

Appendix 2: *Gandhi* in America

I went to the American Consulate in Vancouver, Canada, for a visa. The officer looked at my passport and said, "This has been issued in Chennai. We can issue a visa to you only after we hear from Chennai that there is no objection to your going to America." Since correspondence by post would take a long time, I requested them to send a telegram at my expense. The reply that there was no objection came in four days.

Since my passport specified journalism as my profession, they said at the consulate, "We have to write to the Home Department, Washington, and only on their approval can we issue a visa for you."

I asked, "How many days will that take?"

"Not less than eight weeks."

This 'special treatment' was reserved for all foreign journalists.

After making repeated phone calls to Washington, the Home Department replied at last. Since the reply was favourable, I was issued a visa permitting a three-month stay in America. And I had to pay two dollars for that—almost ten rupees. Besides that, they took my fingerprints as if I were a convict.

Obtaining the visa was not enough. One can enter America only after getting permission from the American Immigration Registration Office. This office was not bound to permit me just because I had obtained a visa. There had been a few cases of refusal. One had to hope that the priest would not snatch away the blessing that God had offered!

When I went to the immigration office, there was only one junior officer. He asked me to come the next day. When I explained that I had already waited for several weeks for the visa, he said, "All the senior officers are out. I don't have the authority to issue the permit. However, I will give you a letter. Go to the address mentioned in it, pay eight dollars and get a receipt. Only on the production of that receipt will the railway authorities issue a travel ticket to you. But that is not enough, come here tomorrow to get the permit."

I acted according to his directions. I went to the specified address, and paid eight dollars (approximately forty rupees). This 'head tax' was imposed on foreigners who stayed for more than thirty days on American soil. I showed the receipt and purchased a rail ticket to San Francisco which cost me almost a hundred rupees.

I went back to the immigration office the next day. The lady there looked into the daily register and said, "You cannot meet the officer this week. I can give you an appointment for next week."

When I described my situation, she consulted the officer and said, "We have given appointments to three people today. If one of them doesn't turn up, we will call you."

God answered my prayers. One of them did not turn up and I was called in.

There were two officers and a woman typist. I was asked to sit down and then administered an oath.

One of the officers said, "Has a friend or a lawyer come with you? They can be your witness." He spoke with a stern expression on his face.

I said, "I have come alone," and handed over the filled application.

The officer dictated the particulars to the typist. In my application, I had indicated my date of birth as 4–11–1911. He read it out as 11 April 1911. I intervened and said that I was born on 4 November 1911.

The officer was taken aback at my objecting to my date of birth. "Isn't that what you have written?" he asked.

"What I've written is correct. But you have read it wrongly." I explained the difference between the Indian and American ways of marking dates. "We write the day first, while you write the month first. I was not born on 11 April, but on 4 November."

Everyone laughed. The officer read out my birth date correctly.

His face turned stern again. The atmosphere became tense, it felt as though we were in a court of law. He cross-examined me for about half an hour. I felt vexed and upset.

The woman did not type everything verbatim. She typed only what the officer wanted her to take down. The important questions and answers were:

Q: Have you ever been in jail?

A: Yes.

Q: Why were you in jail?

A: I did not wish to be in jail. But the then British government put me in jail.

Q: What for?

A: For political reasons.

Q: Are you a communist?

A: No.

Q: Do you have any intention of opposing the American government in a violent manner?

A: No. Definitely not.

Q: Why are you going to America?

A: To produce the English version of my film on Gandhiji.

Q: Have you made any arrangements with anybody?

A: No.

Q: What will you do if you are not able to produce the film?

A: I will go back home.

Q: Do you have enough money to go back?

A: Yes, I do.

Q: Let me see.

After counting the travellers cheques, he said, "Wait outside. We will discuss your case and let you know."

I waited outside—like a criminal awaiting the verdict of the judge.

The door opened. The officer came out and said, "We will issue a permit for you to stay in America for three months if you can pay a deposit of five hundred dollars."

I asked, "Would it be enough if a local person stands surety for the amount?"

"No, you must pay in cash. Pay the money at one of the approved firms on this list."

The manager of the firm that I approached said that I must pay fifteen dollars as fee for the safekeeping of my five hundred dollars free of interest. So I paid five hundred and fifteen dollars and got a receipt. And then I was given the letter of permission.

Later, I came to know that the difficulties I had encountered were much less compared to the difficulties faced by others. Immigration officials had made some unfortunate applicants pay security deposits up to three thousand dollars.

An Indian living in British Guyana went to London via New York. The flight reached New York in the evening. The connecting flight to London was in the following morning. Immigration officials did not allow him to get down. Even though the airlines stood surety for him, American immigration officials appointed a plainclothes policeman to keep watch over the traveller. When he was inside his hotel room, the policeman would stand guard outside. Wherever he went, the policeman would follow him. Until he boarded the flight the next morning, they treated him like a criminal.

They treated an officer of the Indian government, travelling from England to Canada via New York, in a similar manner. Even Europeans and South Americans, and travellers from other countries, have been subjected to cruel and humiliating treatment in the hands of American immigration officials.

The 'petty' immigration officials had the authority to deny permits to travellers coming with visas obtained from the American Consulate. They had unlimited powers. They were not obliged to give any reason for their actions. They protected themselves under that umbrella term 'security'.

The ordeals faced by travellers due to conflicts between the American State Department and Home Department defy description. As a result, America is losing thousands of friends.

~

It took two months for the negative of the Gandhi film to reach Hollywood from Bombay. I stayed in San Francisco till then.

As soon as the film arrived, I left for Hollywood. Thereafter, I had to shuttle between Hollywood and San Francisco.

~

I went to the Indian Consulate in San Francisco. I found that the consul did not come to work everyday. There were two Tamil speakers working in the consulate. Is there anything sweeter than speaking in one's own mother tongue?

I requested help from one of the officers. The railway officials had handed over the box containing the Gandhi film directly to me. Usually they forward it to customs officials who would assess the duty to be paid and forward it to the censor board. It is proper to screen the film only after getting the permission of the censor board. I suspected that the railway officer had absent-mindedly given me the film box. I wanted someone from the consulate to talk to the customs officials and clarify the matter.

If I screened the film without getting the approval of the censor board, newspapers would report that an Indian had acted improperly, not that an individual had committed a mistake. I was determined that no bad name should accrue to India on my account. The customs officials assured my friend from the consulate that there would be no problems.

I questioned him further, "All right. Should I not have an acknowledgement for having brought the film into this country? Otherwise, wouldn't there be trouble when I'm taking it back?"

The consulate officer telephoned again and confirmed that there would be no problem in taking the film out of America, and if questioned, I should say that it was produced in India.

But, a few months later, when the negative of the Gandhi film came to Los Angeles from India, a copy of the negative was made under the supervision of the customs officials. The censor board viewed the film and only then did they hand over the negative to me.

When I was in the Fiji Islands, I had read about the inauguration of the American Academy of Asian Studies in San Francisco, in an American newspaper. I wrote a letter congratulating the president of the association,

Louis P. Gainsborough. In his reply, he said that he had faith in Gandhism and had thus been motivated to start the association. He requested me to meet him if I should ever visit San Francisco.

Gainsborough was a Jew. He was about fifty-five and was handsome in appearance. Since he had begun to work at an early age he had not had much school education.

Jews experienced many disadvantages in America. Overcoming them all, he had earned great wealth. When he was sick and bedridden for a year, he had read books on Indian philosophy and Gandhiji's autobiography. He venerated Gandhiji and the Buddha.

On his recovery, he scaled down the volume of his business and started the American Academy of Asian Studies in a building that he owned. The academy was not oriented towards religion, but served the cause of knowledge.

Initially, Dr. Spiegelberg was the chief professor. Alan Watts, the famous English writer, Sir C.P. Ramaswamy Iyer, Dr. Haridas Chaudhuri, Dr. Mrs. Judith Tyberg, Professor Minto, the Japanese Tokwan Tada who was inducted as a lama after a stay of nine years in Tibet, and others, taught in the academy.

C.P. Ramaswamy Iyer gave lectures on epics twice a week. Drawn by his oratorical skills a number of students attended his classes.

Courses were offered on religions like Hinduism, Islam, Zoroastrianism and Jainism. Languages like Hindi, Urdu, Persian, Chinese, Malay, Bengali and Tamil were also taught. Gurusamy, a young man from Coimbatore, was the Tamil teacher.

The famous teacher Rome Landov, Madam Boon who belonged to the royal family of Thailand, Dilip Kumar Ray of Aurobindo Ashram, and Dr. Malalasekara of the University of Ceylon, had been faculty of this academy for a few months.

Gainsborough saw the Gandhi film along with the students of the academy. He said that since Gandhiji's principles had inspired the founding of the academy, it would be appropriate for the academy to produce the English version of the film. He felt that God must share the wish.

The next day, he asked me to show the film to his friend Werner Johnson, a Hollywood music composer.

Hollywood is about four hundred miles from San Francisco. There is no railway station in Hollywood! To go to Hollywood one must get down at Pasadena or Los Angeles and travel by motorcar.

I remembered Ram Bagai, an Indian friend in Hollywood. Ram's father was a Punjabi. He had settled there with his family. I sent a telegram to Ram about my arrival the next morning.

The train took ten hours and it was a tiring journey. Ram Bagai received me very warmly. More than fourteen years had passed since I met him. But I could not find any change in his physical appearance. He was very happy about the production of the Gandhi film.

We had breakfast on the way and then went to Hotel Roosevelt, the largest hotel in Hollywood. I thought it would be a convenient place for meeting friends.

Since it was morning, I wanted to have a bath. Only if we paid five or six dollars could we get bath facilities. Since I wanted to return the same day, I did not wish to spend so much money. As Ram's house was far off and as he had some other work, I could not go there.

We went to the Hollywood Young Men's Christian Association that was situated nearby. The clerk there welcomed us very kindly. A board there announced 'Membership fee for one day: 75 cents'. One could use the swimming pool and the gym as well. The arrangement was for the convenience of out-of-town visitors who were not members.

I said to the clerk, "I want to become a one-day member."

He laughed and asked, "Do you want to bathe?"

I said, "Yes."

"You, who have come such a long way from India, are welcome to have a bath. It is enough if you pay 10 cents for the soap and towel.'

Ram took leave of me saying that he would be back by eleven.

After my bath, I thanked the clerk. He was an Englishman who had served the army in the Punjab before the war. He described with gratitude the kindness shown to him by Indians.

As soon as Ram arrived, we headed for the Consolidated Film Laboratories. It was a large organisation consisting of many studios and all the facilities, including laboratories, necessary for the film industry. Even producers who had their own studios made use of the laboratories here when they required a large number of prints. It was said to be the biggest of its kind.

There were many floors. We went to the floor where Werner Johnson was shooting, and he received us cordially. That day, Johnson was acting in his own film and was in full make-up. We watched the shooting till noon.

During the lunch interval, Johnson saw the Gandhi film along with his friend Stanley Neal and another person, Edith Martin. It contained three 16 mm reels. The second reel got over and there was nobody to turn off the projector even after a couple of minutes. I went out and looked for the projectionist. I could not find him, but I found four or five employees doing other work.

I addressed one of them, "Could you please stop this projector and run the last reel."

One of them turned off the projector and said, "This is not our work. The projectionist alone can change the reel, I will be fined if I touch it. It is a union regulation."

It took some time for the projectionist to come back. We waited until then.

After the film was screened, Ram left me again saying that he would return by six in the evening.

I spent the whole day in the shooting area. Tourists who visit Hollywood in thousands are crazy about watching film shootings. Occasionally, permission is given to enter the shooting floors. But normally nobody is permitted to remain. I lingered, as I had nowhere else to go.

There was no dearth of food in the studio, especially in locations where work was taking place. There was hot coffee as well as a number of paper cups. The workers could measure out coffee decoction in desired quantities and add sugar and milk. Americans substituted thick cream for milk. There were also doughnuts and a variety of cakes and sandwiches. Anybody could take as much as they wished.

Werner Johnson was one of the popular music composers of America. That day they were producing a 16 mm–colour musical for school students in a grand manner. Whatever the size of the film, 16 mm or 35 mm, the settings and lighting are the same. Only two actors and two actresses were working. There were two or three scene settings.

During the shooting, one could find no difference between the proprietor and the employees. I was amazed to observe all the workers engaging themselves in the work in unison and not trying to find fault with one another. They did not waste even a single minute. Their sense of duty pleased me. America's inexhaustible asset is the untiring work of its people.

~

At the stroke of six, everyone stopped their work and left. Ram had not returned. Most of the workers owned cars. A few offered to take me with them. I thanked them for their kindness and waited for Ram.

Werner Johnson took leave of me saying that he would convey his opinion to Gainsborough.

Ram came for me after a little while. He said, "Let us go home for dinner. I will drop you at the station later. This is my wife's command."

After dinner, Ram took me to the station. He told me that he did not expect any favourable opinion from Werner Johnson about the film. He saw me off with a cheerful face.

Since I had no urgent work in San Francisco, I decided to spend a day at Stockton.

I could not sleep on the train. That night, as usual, I wrote the day's accounts—the whole day had only cost ten cents. Just ten cents for staying a whole day in Hollywood, travelling several miles by car and finishing all my work!

Very few people in the world work as fast as the Americans once they get interested. Werner Johnson spoke to Gainsborough over the phone the very night he saw the film. Following Gainsborough's proposal, Johnson and Neal came to San Francisco the next morning by flight. They had decided to produce the film. They were waiting for me!

We agreed that Stanley Neal would produce the film. Since he desired that I should remain in America and help him until the work was completed, arrangements were made for my stay.

~

Hollywood is the international film capital. But most of the studios are located in nearby towns. Actors and actresses live in Beverly Hills.

The shooting area in a studio is called the 'stage'. Large studios have many stages. A scene is shot from several angles. At times, a scene is shot twice or thrice. The one found most suitable is included in the film.

After the shooting is over the film reels are sent to the laboratory for processing. At this stage the film reel is called a 'negative'. The copy made from it is the 'positive'.

The positive reel is subjected to careful examination. The required sections are cut and spliced to align with the narration of the story. The final copy, since it has to be completely satisfactory, takes shape only after several alterations.

Once the recording of sound is over, the film reel becomes a sound negative. Copies made from this are 'sound positives'.

The sound positive is processed so that it matches the final copy of the mute print—the words must synchronise with lip movement.

The exact portions of the negative film reels matching with the 'married print' (positive copy of a film bearing both picture and sound in synchronisation) are identified, cut and spliced together. Copies are then made as per requirement using both the negatives.

All the works connected with the film reel – such as cutting, splicing, and synchronising sound with picture – are done in the editing room. Among the many devices in an editing room the most important is the movieola. It is not easy to screen a film for viewing again and again. Even if it is screened, it may not be possible to stop it at the required place and make corrections. When the reel is run on a movieola, one or two people can easily view the picture. It is easy to run the film at any speed and it can also be run forward or backward. The film can also be stopped instantaneously. Sound positive film reels too may be run on a movieola and recorded sounds can be heard precisely. A movieola is indispensable for film production of exacting standards.

In an editing room there are tables fitted with instruments for cutting and splicing film reels, for winding and unwinding them, and machines for synchronising sound. The person who discharges the editing room work ably is the 'editor'.

~

The film production was to be done at the Hal Roach Studios. In American parlance, a studio is a 'lot'. I asked someone, "How good is that studio?"

The person replied, "It is small among large studios, but large among small studios." He could have said it in two words: medium size.

Hal Roach Studios was located in Culver City. It took an hour to reach the studio by bus from where I stayed. The fare was 60 cents up and down—a little more than three rupees.

Two film journals – *Hollywood* and *Variety* – were published from Hollywood. They were printed on superior art paper, on four pages, and cost a cent each.

When I went to Hal Roach Studios for the first time the watchman was very strict with me. When I told him that I wanted to go to the office of Neal Pictures, he called them over the phone and only then did he take me there.

Inside the studio, a large area was set apart for parking nearly fifty cars. The space allotted for the watchman's car was marked with white lines.

A studio is usually not reserved for the exclusive use of the owner. It can also be rented out. More than ten offices of various film companies functioned from inside Hal Roach. Neal Pictures was one of them. Its head quarters was in New York and it had a branch in Chicago. Mrs. D'Worth was the secretary of the Hollywood branch.

~

Mrs. Edith Martin had about twenty-five years of experience in film production. She had produced many commercials and a few documentaries. She said that the documentary on Gandhiji was going to be the most important project of her life.

Documentaries are not based on imaginary stories like other films, but on true happenings. They are films that improve knowledge. Documentaries make it possible for us to witness events of the past.

Documentaries were born at the same time as feature films. They are produced by collating events that happened in various parts of the world. Normally, a documentary runs for about ten minutes.

In 1920, when Bal Gangadhar Tilak died, lakhs of people took part in the funeral procession. A documentary was made on Tilak's funeral procession. This is apparently the first documentary produced in India.

Earlier the English and the French had produced documentaries in India. A Frenchman had filmed Gandhiji addressing a meeting wearing a shirt and a cap.

Though the first documentary was produced in 1920, no one in India repeated the effort. Now and then some important events were filmed. Some of them were connected with the nationalist movement.

The documentary on Mahatma Gandhi was produced by collecting stock shots from the documentaries produced in India and other foreign countries, of Gandhiji's movements and activities, and by adding new shots of his later life.

This was produced with commentaries in Tamil, Telugu and Hindi. Based on this version, we began working on the production of the English version in America.

~

A cutting-room was hired in Hal Roach Studios. Robert Warwick was the film editor. He was a Mexican and his wife was an American.

Bob was an expert cinematographer with twenty-five years of experience in film production. He said that he had been denied membership in the cinematographers union because he was a Mexican and that it was with great difficulty that he had joined the editors union.

Bob was a man of fine qualities. Nothing could distract him from performing his duty. Since he was born in Mexico, he was familiar with independence movements. Edith Martin said that we were fortunate to have the capable Bob as our editor.

The editor was paid a salary of 350 dollars a week. An assistant editor was to be appointed a week after the work had begun. He had to be a member of the union and his salary was fixed at 150 dollars per week.

First, Bob cut all the positive film rolls, scene by scene, and classified and numbered them. This took a week.

Edith Martin did her work mostly in the cutting-room. Her job was only to issue instructions and she could not touch the film. The regulations of the union permit only the editor and his assistant to handle the film in the cutting-room.

~

There were two preview theatres in the studio. Once, during a screening, a film reel snapped apart. When I requested the projectionist to splice the film, he said, "According to union regulations I should not touch the film reel. Only the editor can do that."

I pleaded with him, "I am a stranger to this place. Won't you kindly help me?"

He explained to me patiently, "I wish I could. But I am sorry, I cannot splice the film. This film reel is under production. The editor might have completed the track-laying. Splicing will reduce the length of the film and the synchronisation will be disturbed. But the editor can do it without causing any damage. If anybody interferes in another's work it will only lead to unnecessary loss and waste of time. If a person does the work all by himself, it will lead to orderliness and excellence. Regulations are there for specific reasons."

They edited the scene showing Gandhiji's arrival in Bombay from London. Mustn't there be a huge crowd at the time Gandhiji disembarked? From the shots classified as "crowds" they chose one and inserted it. Only when I saw it on screen did I notice that it was a Chennai crowd. I identified a replacement shot showing the Bombay crowd.

I explained to the editor, "The distance between Los Angeles and New York is 3200 miles. Crowds of these two cities wouldn't appear any different from one another. It would be the same in whichever American state you may shoot. Throughout your country, people wear the same kind of clothes. But in India, people clothe themselves differently in each state."

He was surprised to hear that people wear different kinds of clothes within a single country!

Once when Bob was seriously engaged in work, I invited him to have a cup of coffee.

He said, "It would take away ten minutes. Work should not be interrupted. Let's have coffee after finishing work. I am sorry." I was struck by his sense of duty.

~

We had to take shots of the Bible and the Gita for the film.

Edith Martin said, "I need a copy of the Gita in Sanskrit and a Bible with an ornate cover."

I had no trouble in getting the Gita. The place where I stayed was a veritable library. There were more than a thousand books belonging to Dr Govinda Puttaiah. I got a copy of the Gita from him.

But I could not get a Bible with an ornate cover though I searched Los Angeles and Hollywood for three days. I even looked for such a copy in three churches.

I got the address of a Bible publishing society and located it after a three-hour search. I met the manager of the society and said, "We are producing a documentary on Gandhiji. I request you to lend us a Bible with a beautiful cover. I will return it as soon as the shooting is over."

He said, "You appear to be an honest person. Generally, we do not trust people associated with films. Once, a film person borrowed a Bible, but he did not return it."

He thought for a while and said, "The price of the Bible is twelve dollars. If you deposit that amount I will give you a copy. You can get the money back when you return the book."

I agreed.

On seeing the Bible he brought, I was thoroughly disappointed. The front cover was good but there were no pictures.

I thanked him and left. I often recollect what he said about people associated with films. It seems they are trusted in no country!

❧

What kind of background music should we use for the film? If a music troupe were engaged exclusively for this film, the expenses would be prohibitive. I was told that only canned music was used even for the documentary, *The Roosevelt Story,* made on the American president.

In America there is a music centre where the recorded collections of concerts of popular music composers are available. After paying a nominal fee one could make copies of whatever music that was suitable. This would bring down our expenses considerably.

But Gainsborough did not like this idea. He wanted the film to be excellent in every aspect. He appointed the famous Edward Paul as the music director.

American trade unions do not permit the use of music produced anywhere outside America. If anybody violated the code, the Union of Theatre Employees would refuse to screen the film.

In our film we had to use Indian music in certain scenes. For that we got permission from the Union of Cinema Music Composers.

The narrator for the Gandhi film had to be of high repute. One of the most popular narrators of Hollywood came forward to do it without remuneration. He asked us to send a copy of the commentary to him and another to his agent. The agent wanted us to send a copy of the commentary to the Institute of Motion Picture Co-ordination. He wrote that the narrator could undertake the job only if they approved the script.

In America, actors, actresses, music directors and narrators function only through agents. Since it would be difficult for each of them to employ and pay for an agent exclusively there are numerous agents bureaus in America.

If a producer wants an actor to act in his film, he goes to the actor's agent. The agent negotiates with the producer and fixes the fee to be paid to the actor, and the mode of payment. He also ensures that the terms of the contract are not injurious to the actor's interests. Further, the agent sees to it that the actor is given due importance in the film's advertisements and that the money agreed upon is paid as per the contract. For his work, the agent charges a small percentage of the actor's fee. Of course, the agent makes a commitment only after getting the concurrence of the actor.

The contract specifies the importance to be given to the actor even in the credits on the title cards shown at the opening of a film. Generally, there are separate cards for the name of the studio, the title of the film, the director and the producer of the film. A single card is allowed for the technical experts like the cinematographer, the recordist and the laboratory head, and their assistants. Very popular actors and actresses get separate title cards. All others are grouped together in one card. The names of some popular artistes are given in bold letters. Famous music directors too get separate title cards.

It is the job of the agent to ensure that the name of the actor figures in the title card as per the contract.

~

There was no censor board attached to the government that monitored films produced in America. The producers adhered to a self-imposed code.

I heard that the Institute of Motion Pictures Co-ordination had links with the government. Producers had to submit stories, scripts and songs to the institute and begin production only after getting its approval. This process could take several months. This approval is tantamount to censorship—one way of preventing the spread of communism.

No actor or actress would work for a film that had not received the institute's approval, for the reason that they might be branded communist or anti-national.

Quentin Reynolds, a famous American writer and radio critic, was finally appointed as the narrator. He came to Hollywood from New York for this purpose. His visit was publicised in the newspapers as an important event.

Quentin Reynolds saw the film before attempting the narration. After the show was over, he came out with tears in his eyes and said, "I know that Mahatma Gandhi was a great man. I have read the book authored by Vincent Sheean. But having watched this film, I understand now, that the Mahatma was an exceptionally great man."

Quentin Reynolds' narration matched Edith Martin's commentary. It took two days to complete the recording. There were more than sixty Sanskrit words and Indian names. Dr. Govinda Puttaiah trained Reynolds to pronounce those words correctly.

The production of the film came to an end. I left after seeing the release copy.

On reaching my place of residence, I received a telephone call from Vancouver. Kartar Singh, one of the Indian leaders in Canada, had called to enquire how I was.

"The film has been completed. I have just returned home after seeing it. By God's grace, it has come out well."

Kartar Singh said, "I know the film will be good. But how is your financial situation?"

"I have absolutely no money."

He said, "I'll wire money to your San Francisco address tomorrow."

A few days ago, I had received a telegram from Vancouver: "Help arriving. Sri Ramajayam." My friend Adimoola Murthy who knew about my financial condition had sent it.

On seeing the words 'Sri Ramajayam' I felt a thrill run through my body. I rejoiced, recognising it as help from God.

After the completion of the film I left Hollywood for San Francisco the very next day.

The Indian ambassador to America made arrangements for screening the film in Washington on 10 February 1953.

I made arrangements with the help of a few friends in California to go to Washington first and then to New York by air.

California had been my home for a year.

My ticket to New York was booked on the midnight flight of 7 February. It was a low-priced tourist flight that took eighteen hours. A friend dropped me off at the airport before 10 p.m.

The airport was huge. It had facilities for the comfortable stay of hundreds of passengers. There were all kinds of machines dispensing chocolates, cigarettes, cold drinks, hot coffee, chewing gums, etc.

Likewise, there was a machine for vending insurance policies: What to do in case of an accident while on the flight? A policy document slides out when the specified amount of money is dropped into the slot provided in the machine. The value of a policy is five thousand dollars. To insure for twenty-five thousand dollars one must fill out five policy documents. All this is done in a matter of seconds. The number of the policy is printed at the end of the policy document and is easily detached. This portion is the receipt. The buyer retains it and deposits the policy document in the slot provided in the machine.

There is no agent or clerk. No commission or any bother. Anybody can insure for whatever amount. I saw many people filling insurance forms.

~

In America, before making an air trip all details regarding the date of travel, departure time and the name of the airline are confirmed in writing, well in advance. Yet, on arriving at a particular place, Americans confirm their next journey over phone. It is not obligatory to do that, but it is appreciated. There is no last minute uncertainty whether the passenger will turn up. If one is unable to make the trip and informs the company, it can allot the ticket to waitlisted passengers. Is it not a great help?

In Chicago airport I confirmed my journey at the office of the airline company and deposited my baggage.

The flight departed at midnight. There were only ten passengers while the plane's capacity was sixty.

We reached Denver at 8 o'clock next morning. It was snowing. The whole area looked like it had been covered with a vast white sheet. Sunlight in

San Francisco; snow in Denver. Since the runway was completely covered with snow, I was a little scared when the plane landed.

From Denver I went to Chicago. The Chicago airport was also huge. It took an hour to reach the city by bus.

Palmer House is one of the largest hotels in Chicago. Mumtaz Kitchlew ran a shop selling Indian goods in the basement of the hotel.

Mumtaz was a relative of Dr. Saifuddin Kitchlew, one of the leaders of the Indian Congress. Mumtaz Kitchlew had arrived in America twenty years ago as a student. He had then married an American woman. They were a kind and hospitable couple.

I left Chicago by the midnight flight and reached Washington at three in the morning.

My plan was to leave for New York at midnight after the screening. I would be charged two days' rent in a hotel if I stayed from three in the morning until midnight. I was not sure how much it would cost me. In view of my financial condition, I decided not to rent a room.

I went to the top floor of the airport building. It was spacious. At that time it was quiet. Won't there be at least a few people like me? I saw two passengers dozing comfortably on sofas. I too slept on a sofa.

I got up at six and finished my morning ablutions. That huge airport had all kinds of facilities, but none for bathing.

I deposited my luggage in the airport office and went out for breakfast. I had to wait till seven for the restaurant to open. Like me, an American youth was also waiting. He had returned to his mother country after serving in the American air force, in England, for two years. He had not liked England at all. He kept making fun of the bland food of the English. He was sickened by the very thought of the mist in England.

We ate breakfast together. He was delighted to eat American food after two years. He insisted on my being his guest as I had come from a foreign country.

From the airport I went to the Indian Embassy by bus.

Professor Sundaram welcomed me cheerfully with the words: "The president of the United States of America is going to see your film today." Sundaram was the educational officer of the embassy.

Then I met Bhandari, the public relations officer. He had ensured good publicity for the Gandhi film in newspapers during the past two weeks.

He said, "We sent invitations to a number of people. A few wrote back expressing their inability to attend the screening. The president's participation was confirmed only four days ago. This news spread and even those who had expressed their inability to come have since changed their minds. The auditorium can accommodate only four hundred people. Since we have a large number of guests, we have invited only a few Indians. Please be present at 8.30."

The invitation card specified "Dress – Black Tie". The dress code emphasised the importance and significance of the programme. The audience had to come in special evening dress to see the film on Mahatma Gandhi who wore only a loin-cloth!

Indians could choose between formal evening dress and the national dress of India. I told Bhandari that I had neither. He said, "You need not worry about it. You can come in ordinary clothes, just like what you are wearing now."

In 1939, when we filmed Gandhiji at Wardha, Dr. Peter Booke, an American, was staying there. We had filmed him taking a stroll with Gandhiji. Every time I saw that scene I was reminded of him.

I had lost his address. Fortunately, when I was in Canada I tracked down his address through a friend.

Booke was living in Cincinnati, seven hundred miles from Washington. On my request, the Indian ambassador sent invitations to Dr. and Mrs. Booke. Dr. Peter Booke alone came for the screening.

Next in rank to the ambassador was the first secretary, Bahadur Singh. He was born in Trinidad. I knew him, so I had lunch with him. He introduced his colleagues to me.

The Indian Ambassador Jagan Viharilal Mehta invited me to tea that evening. We conversed for about half an hour.

Many Indians could not get an invitation for the show. I could take only one guest. A few people earnestly requested me to take them. I told one of them who was already known to me, "I'll take you to the show on one condition. You must help me find a place to have a bath."

The friend agreed readily. We went to his house. His wife provided me a tasty vegetarian meal of sambar, rasam, appalam, payasam, curds and pickle with rice.

My friend and I reached the Dupont Theatre exactly at 8.30 p.m. It was a popular but small theatre.

Two Sikhs, majestic in military uniform, stood at the entrance.

An Indian art exhibition had recently concluded in Washington. The theatre was therefore decorated with important artefacts brought from the exhibition. A small and beautiful statuette of Gandhiji and the tricolour flag of India were displayed in an aesthetic manner.

Guests began arriving one by one. General Carlos P. Romulo, who was the president of the United Nations Organisation, his wife, and the Russian Ambassador Andrei Gromyko came for the screening.

Press correspondents, photographers and reporters came in large numbers. I learnt that the intelligence branch of the American police were also there for security reasons.

The theatre was full by 8.50 p.m. President Eisenhower, his wife and their retinue arrived at 8.55 p.m. The manager of the theatre led the president and his wife in. The Indian Ambassador Mehta and his daughter Aparna welcomed the presidential couple. Aparna presented the first lady a beautiful bouquet.

Mr. and Mrs. President sat amidst the audience. There was neither a special place nor special seats for them.

The Indian Ambassador Mehta spoke a few words in praise of the greatness of the Mahatma and welcomed the presidential couple and the others. Then the show began.

Only twenty days had passed since the president had assumed office. That was his first public appearance. All the eminent personalities of Washington were present. In Washington – perhaps in the whole of America – that was the day's most important event.

The ambassadors of Afghanistan, Argentina, Burma, Ceylon, Denmark, Indonesia, Iran, Israel, Mexico, the Philippines, Poland, Saudi Arabia, Thailand, Soviet Russia, Yugoslavia, Switzerland, Iraq, Jordan, Luxemburg,

Syria, Nepal and Yemen, and the representatives of many other countries came with their families to attend the show.

American senators William F. Noland, Paul H. Douglas, Theodore Greene, K.M. Gillet and Homer Ferguson, the Education Secretary Margaret, and the director of the Library of Congress, Evans Walter Lipman, had also come with their families.

The actresses Shirley Temple and Mirina Loy had also come. Their husbands were top officials in Washington. Shirley Temple later became Mrs. Black, and Myrna Loy, Mrs. Sergeant.

The show came to an end at 10.30 p.m. The audience remained in their seats calmly until Mr. and Mrs. President left.

I took leave of the Indian ambassador and other friends. The friend who accompanied me to the screening drove me to the airport.

On the way to the Washington airport I enjoyed seeing various parts of the city and the lifelike statue of Abraham Lincoln.

There were flights from Washington to New York every fifteen minutes in the morning, every thirty minutes in the afternoon and every one hour in the night. The journey took forty-five minutes.

But I was not sure whether I could spend the night in the New York airport as I had in Washington. I decided to take the morning flight and therefore slept in the same place as the night before.

I got up early in the morning and read the morning papers. Later, I read the evening papers too. The popular *Washington Post* had set apart half a page for the Gandhi film. All the newspapers had published photographs.

The names of the people who attended the show, their clothes, the beauty of their jewels and the varieties of flowers worn by them were described in detail. The convention was to publish reviews only after a film had been screened in public. Contrary to this practice, a woman correspondent had written in her half-page article: "At the end of this moving picture very few eyes were without tears."

From *America Naattil*
1956, Chennai

Index